The New Mediterranean Table

PAGE STREET
PUBLISHING CO.

First published in 2015 by
Page Street Publishing Co.
27 Congress Street, Suite 103
Salem, MA 01970
www.pagestreetpublishing.com

Distributed by Macmillan; sales in Canada by The Canadian Manda Group.

18 17 16 15 2 3 4 5

ISBN-13: 978-1-62414-095-2
ISBN-10: 1-62414-095-5

Library of Congress Control Number: 2014950215

Cover and book design by Page Street Publishing Co.
Photography by Matt Lien

Printed and bound in U.S.A.

Page Street is proud to be a member of 1% for the Planet. Members donate one percent of their
sales to one or more of the over 1,500 environmental and sustainability charities across the globe
who participate in this program.

The New Mediterranean Table

Modern and Rustic Recipes Inspired by Cooking Traditions
Spanning Three Continents

Sameh Wadi

Chef/owner of the critically acclaimed and award-winning
Saffron Restaurant and Lounge in Minneapolis

PAGE STREET
PUBLISHING CO.

To My Father

In my heart and mind you are still here, guiding and pushing me to be audacious. I hope to continue your legacy. You are my idol.

To My Mother

Your passion and adoration have been continually motivating, inspiring me to become a better person and chef. I love you more than I can express here.

Contents

Introduction

My roots are Mediterranean, influencing my love and appreciation for its cuisine. It is food that expresses the spirit of my ancestors. I have embraced its rich ingredients and traditional techniques, and it has shaped my philosophy about food. The cuisine is about coaxing complex flavors and harmonizing ingredients to make vibrant and robust dishes. This food is to be made with passion and soul, and it is best when enjoyed with loved ones. Mediterranean cuisine connects me to my heritage and the bold essence of its culture.

Traditionally speaking, Mediterranean cuisine is the food from the cultures adjacent to the Mediterranean Sea. Although this region spans a wide variety of ethnicities, religions and climates, strong historical connections and the nomadic nature of its early inhabitants led to common elements and undertones in the foods.

For many years, the main focus of Mediterranean cuisine has been on the foods of Italy, Spain and the south of France. It wasn't until recently that a growing interest in eastern Mediterranean cuisine started to take place. In the culinary world, more chefs began to experiment with these exotic flavors and incorporate spices from the eastern Mediterranean into American and European kitchens. Simultaneously, ingredients like hummus and Greek yogurt have worked their way into Western homes.

One of the pillars of Mediterranean cuisine is the use and balance of intricate spices. I can no longer imagine cuisine without them. The culinary world would be a dull place had we not been introduced to their mystical, alluring and transformative properties. I believe in the language of spices. Each one conveys a feeling or evokes an emotion, in the same way that poetry, art or music does.

When I was young, my mother would often recall a story about my *sedo*, grandfather, that reflects the impact of spice. For special occasions and when hosting guests, he would call for the coffee with cardamom and saffron. In these instances, the coffee with spices symbolized gracious hospitality and warmth. In my own cooking, each spice represents a different sensation or sentiment. A romantic at heart, I equate cinnamon with comfort and ginger with passion. I use spices deliberately, always weaving a story with flavor, texture and smell. As I do so, I am mindful that ancient civilizations were formed and empires built around the spice trade. Throughout history, spices symbolized everything from affluence and power to healing and wellness. These same spices today have become a staple in most kitchen pantries and are more commonly used in everyday foods.

Growing up in a household that was passionate about food and culture ignited my interest in cooking and eating. Every meal was a social event. The whole family was present and, often, in the midst of enjoying one meal, would be discussing the dishes for the next. Every day my mother prepared multiple dishes for lunch and dinner. Extended family and friends would arrive, frequently unannounced. There was always ample and delectable food on the table. In my world, this kind of hospitality was normal; this was the way of life.

In the late 1980s, my parents, along with my uncle, started to compile and write recipes for a cookbook titled *The Encyclopedia of Palestinian Cuisine*, a collection of traditional recipes and dishes that embodied the cuisine of their homeland–Palestine. Once word got out about their effort, letters and recipes started to arrive from Palestinians all around the world. There was a movement to share stories to preserve time-honored tradition through food.

During those years, I remember waking up in the morning to the smell of food wafting out of the kitchen. I recall walking into the dining room to find my dad and uncle setting up their studio for the day, getting the props ready for the photo shoot. My mother would be in the kitchen, testing the recipes and plating the food.

Then, in 1990, before the book could get to print, my family was forced to relocate as a result of the Gulf War. The book never did get published. Several years ago, my brother, Saed, found the complete manuscript of the book in storage. It had survived three moves across the world. Reading this manuscript not only brought back memories, but it also inspired me to dig deeper into my history. I found recipes that influenced my current culinary style and translated into dishes that are included in this cookbook.

I have been repeatedly asked to define my style of cooking. It is one of the most difficult questions for me to answer. For the past thirteen years of cooking professionally, I have been developing my style as a chef. I weave bold flavors and spices from the old world with local ingredients while using both classic and current techniques to create dishes that capture the essence of the Mediterranean. My fascination for Middle Eastern foods came from being surrounded by vivid flavors from childhood. More recently, I have developed an affinity for the familiar yet unusual flavors of North Africa.

On a personal note, it has been a lifelong goal of mine to engage people in experiencing this rich culture through the diverse and vibrant flavors of the region. I consider myself an ambassador of my culture and heritage—a translator of old-world cuisine to everyday cooking.

I understand and respect tradition, and at the same time, appreciate that cuisine evolves and tastes change. Deep down, I am a purist about the classic dishes that I grew up eating. I never want to change those. They need no improving or elevating. They are perfect the way they are.

—Sameh Wadi

المعجنات

المعجنات

طريقة عمل عجينة البطا ؟

المقادير :

- ١ كيلو د قيق
- كوب ماء دفيء
- كوب حليب بودرة
- ٤ بيض
- ملعقة كبيرة سكر
- ملعقة كبيرة خميرة
- نصف كوب زيت
- ملح و ماء

الطريقة : □ نخل الدقيق و ليضاف اليه الملح والخميرة و بسكر والبيض والزيت ثم يغزل الخليط لمدة محم. . .

□ يضاف الماء ثم يمزج تمزج المكونات . . . قرصة العجينة جيدا ويغطى العجينة حتى تكون لمدة ساعتين تقريبا . تلف وتترك في مكان دافئ

□ تقطع قطعة مساوية ويقطر العجين ويعم أو يسلس أو العجين يعدل بالشوبك وتغطى حبك حسب الرغبة ، أو تترك أوراق عذ وتقطع

ملاحظة : يجب علينا التأكد من أن العجينة قد اختمرت تماما قبل عملية العجين يرتفع الحجرة وتنتفخ شم وينساب الزيت وعجين يختم على جوانب العجين .

ABOUT THE BOOK

This book is for anyone who is interested in exploring the rich culinary tradition of the Mediterranean and learning recipes and techniques to make it their own. It is a journey beyond run-of-the-mill recipes. It is a mixture of quick, simple and easy-to-reproduce dishes with basic ingredients and more labor-intensive ones that require patience and practice. It is a perfect balance between recipes for intermediate and avid cooks. Some of these recipes are dishes that were inspired by food from my childhood; some are dishes that I have served or still serve at my restaurant, Saffron; others are riffs on classic dishes that I love.

The book is organized by chapters that flow as a typical meal would in the Mediterranean, from small plates—*mezze* or pre-appetizers—to appetizers and salads to main courses and side dishes, finishing with desserts and drinks. Many recipes have stories; I have included some of those throughout the book. Some are reflections on memories and associated emotions from my childhood, while others offer a glimpse into the mind of a chef.

In honor of the old-world tradition of making everything from scratch, I have included some basic pantry recipes that range from preserving and pickling to making your own yogurt and cheese. While I understand that not everyone has the time to preserve their own lemons, make their own sausage and blend spices, I have included these recipes for the adventurous.

Finally, I had a difficult time deciding which recipes to include in this book. And actually, the hardest part was formulating the recipes themselves. For the most part, when I cook I rely on memory and taste rather than formulas and ratios. Spice blends and baking are the exceptions. I believe that cooking is about trial and error. It is about learning from the mistakes that you make and adjusting. So, as you journey through this cookbook, use these recipes as guidelines. Explore, experiment and create your own interpretations. Add and subtract ingredients to make the dishes your own. Challenge yourself with unfamiliar ingredients, techniques and flavors. Enjoy the taste and aroma of the food as you cook. In the end, while I hope you learn something from these pages, I also hope you fall in love with these flavors as well as the romance and tradition of this amazing cuisine.

WEIGHT AND MEASURING

I rarely measure anything when cooking. When I do, it is by weight—grams, to be exact. It is much more precise, especially when measuring spices and ingredients for baking. I have included both volume (tablespoons and cups) and metric weight and volume (grams and milliliters). I would recommend that you ultimately invest in a scale that reads to single decimals and to exclusively measure spices by weight rather than volume.

INGREDIENTS

As a rule, buy the best-quality ingredients—from spices and vinegar to produce and meat—that you can afford. It will make a difference in the final dishes.

Use neutral oils (grapeseed or canola) with a high smoking point when high-heat cooking. Use extra virgin olive oil for finishing and flavoring. Olive oil refers to "pure" or a blend of refined olive oil with virgin olive oil.

When a recipe calls for sea salt, it means fine sea salt. For kosher salt, I prefer Diamond Crystal. For a crunchy finishing salt, I like to use Maldon because of the large flakes. The majority of the spices throughout are whole, freshly toasted and ground. Spice blends are kept in airtight containers, away from heat, moisture and strong smells.

Small Plates

The recipes in this chapter are about the little bites offered at the start of a meal or gathering. The majority of these dishes are designed for sharing, encouraging you to take part in the communal dining tradition that is customary in the Mediterranean. Several of these recipes are *mezze,* or pre-appetizers; others are composed salads, appetizers and soups. Seasonal, vegetable-based dishes make up the majority of these recipes. They can be easily adapted into side dishes.

Traditionally, an assortment of these small dishes are served together to showcase contrasting flavors and textures in the beginning of the meal, usually with accompanying beverages. Everyone sits around the table and helps themselves to small bites of whatever they like. Sometimes, people forgo main dishes altogether and make a plentiful meal by combining a variety of these dishes.

Baked Giant Beans with Tomato & Dill

This preparation of giant beans, or *gigantes*, is Greek in origin. In this recipe they are paired with tomato sauce that is cooked with cinnamon. When cinnamon is used in savory dishes, it gives the dish warmth and depth. The cooked beans can be used in different ways. A crowd favorite at Saffron is the giant beans simply dressed with lemon juice, olive oil, diced shallots and lots of fresh chopped dill.

8 SERVINGS

FOR THE GIANT BEANS

3 cups (570 g) dried giant beans, rinsed and soaked in water overnight

1 celery stalk

1 handful of fresh dill, thyme and a bay leaf, wrapped into a bundle with kitchen twine

Sea salt

5 tbsp (75 ml) extra virgin olive oil

1 medium onion, finely diced

1½ tsp (3.9 g) ground cinnamon

½ tsp chile flakes

2 tsp (8.4 g) sugar

8 garlic cloves, chopped

3 cups (750 g) San Marzano tomatoes, crushed by hand

2 tbsp (6 g) fresh dill, roughly chopped

TO FINISH

1 cup (150 g) cow's milk feta cheese, crumbled

2 tbsp (57 g) unsalted butter

1 cup (64 g) panko breadcrumbs

Dill leaves, for garnish

Extra virgin olive oil, for garnish

FOR THE GIANT BEANS

Place the giant beans, celery and herb bundle in a large saucepan, cover by 2 inches (5 cm) of water and bring to a boil. Simmer over low heat, stirring occasionally, until the beans are just tender, about 2½–3 hours, adding more water as needed to keep the beans covered by 2 inches (5 cm). Season the cooked beans with a generous amount of salt and refrigerate for 1 hour. They can be reserved under refrigeration for up to 3 days in the liquid at this point.

When ready to use, drain the beans and discard the liquid, celery and herb bundle.

In a medium saucepan, heat the olive oil. Add the onion, season with a small amount of salt and cook over moderately low heat until softened, about 6–7 minutes. Add the cinnamon, chile flakes, sugar, garlic, tomatoes and chopped dill. Season with salt and simmer over moderate heat, stirring occasionally, until the sauce has reduced slightly, about 10 minutes.

TO FINISH

Preheat the oven to 425°F (218°C). In a 13 inch (33 cm) terra-cotta baking dish, mix the cooked beans with the tomato sauce and sprinkle the feta on top. Bake in the upper rack of the oven for about 15–25 minutes, until the beans are bubbling and the cheese is browned. Remove the baking dish from the oven and let stand for 10 minutes.

Meanwhile, in a large skillet, heat the butter until it starts to bubble, then add the breadcrumbs and cook over moderate heat, stirring continuously, until they are toasted and have a deep golden color, about 4–5 minutes. Season with salt and top the beans with the breadcrumbs; garnish with leaves of fresh dill and a drizzle of olive oil.

CHEF'S TIP: When soaking beans, use a container that is at least five times bigger than the amount of beans. Forgot to soak the beans? No problem. Place them in a large saucepan and cover with 3 inches (8 cm) of water. Bring them to a boil, turn off the heat and let them stand in the liquid for 50–60 minutes. Drain the cooking liquid, rinse under cold water and use in the recipe as needed.

Carrot Salad with Grapefruit and Charmoula

This recipe is inspired by one of the most popular Moroccan "7 salads," the ubiquitous carrot and orange salad. Here, thinly sliced carrots are paired with grapefruit slices and charmoula. The sweet and tart flavor of the ruby grapefruit balances the earthy and sweet flavor of the carrots while the charmoula gives them a nudge of flavor and some heat. I love serving this salad as part of a large mezze spread for parties or pairing it with a hearty meat stew.

6–8 SERVINGS

FOR THE CARROT SALAD

1 ruby grapefruit

6–8 heirloom carrots, peeled and very thinly sliced on a Japanese mandoline

3 radishes, very thinly sliced on a Japanese mandoline

2 tbsp (8 g) flat-leaf parsley, roughly chopped

Maldon salt

FOR THE GRAPEFRUIT CHARMOULA DRESSING

1 tbsp (15 ml) fresh lemon juice

1 tbsp (15 ml) grapefruit juice, reserved from cutting grapefruits

2 tbsp (20 g) Charmoula (page 177)

2 tbsp (30 ml) extra virgin olive oil

Sea salt

FOR THE CARROT SALAD

Using a sharp paring knife, peel the grapefruit, removing all of the bitter white pith, then cut between the membranes to release the segments. Cut the grapefruit segments in half and squeeze the peel of the grapefruit over them to keep moist.

In a medium mixing bowl, combine the grapefruit segments and carrots, reserving the grapefruit juice for the grapefruit charmoula dressing.

FOR THE GRAPEFRUIT CHARMOULA DRESSING

In a small mixing bowl, whisk together the lemon juice, reserved grapefruit juice, charmoula and olive oil, season with salt and reserve.

TO PLATE

Arrange the carrots and grapefruit segments on a large platter or individual plates. Drizzle a small amount of the charmoula dressing on top. Garnish with the radishes, parsley and a bit of the crunchy salt.

CHEF'S TIP: I will be honest with you: I can't bring myself to just serve the carrots thinly sliced. I typically soak them in ice water for an hour to help make them curly and crunchy.

Deviled Eggs with Preserved Tuna and Cumin Salt

Growing up, I loved eating hard-boiled eggs with olive oil and cumin salt, and that's where one of the inspirations for this dish came from. The other came from Niçoise salad, which is one of my favorite lunchtime snacks. The high-quality preserved tuna gets mixed with Niçoise olives, piquillo peppers, capers and tarragon and it tops the egg that gets seasoned with the cumin salt. The olives and capers add acidity and brininess, which balances the richness of the tuna.

8 SERVINGS

FOR THE TUNA SALAD

6 ounces (170 g) high-quality preserved tuna in oil, drained

1 piquillo pepper, finely minced

6 Niçoise olives, pitted and finely minced

½ tbsp (4 g) finely minced capers

½ tbsp (5 g) finely minced shallot

½ tbsp (7 ml) good-quality red wine vinegar

1½ tbsp (23 ml) extra virgin olive oil, plus extra for garnish

Sea salt

Freshly ground black pepper

Tarragon leaves, as needed for garnish

FOR THE EGGS & FILLING

8 eggs

¼ cup (63 g) mayonnaise, homemade or store-bought

¼ tsp mustard powder

2 tsp (10 ml) hot sauce, Frank's is recommended

Pinch of cayenne

1 tsp (5 ml) fresh lemon juice

Sea salt

Spice Salt (page 184) made with cumin

FOR THE TUNA SALAD

In a medium bowl, gently toss the preserved tuna with the piquillo peppers, Niçoise olives, capers, shallot, red wine vinegar and olive oil, making sure to leave the tuna in larger chunks. Season with salt and pepper. Can be made a day in advance.

FOR THE EGGS & FILLING

In a medium saucepan, cover the eggs with 1 inch (3 cm) of water and bring to a boil over moderately high heat, reduce the heat to moderate and simmer for 9 minutes. Drain the water and chill the eggs under cold running water in the sink, then peel them under running water and pat them dry with a towel.

Cut the eggs in half lengthwise, remove the yolks, transfer the yolks to a small bowl and mash well with a fork. Stir in the mayonnaise, mustard powder, hot sauce, cayenne and lemon juice. Season with salt and keep mashing until you have a smooth paste.

Season each egg white with a pinch of cumin salt and spoon some of the filling in the middle of the egg white, then top with a spoonful of the tuna salad. Transfer to a serving platter and garnish with the tarragon leaves and a drizzle of olive oil.

CHEF'S TIP: Cut a small sliver off of the bottom of each egg white half, so the eggs can sit on the serving platter without wobbling. At Saffron, we pass the egg filling mixture through a fine-mesh strainer for an ultra-smooth texture.

Charred Fresh Chickpeas with Sea Salt and Lemon

While living in Jordan, I used to go to a street cart in the market and pick up a bush of freshly roasted chickpeas—yes, a bush with all of its leaves and stems. It would be wrapped in a newspaper, sometimes sprinkled with salt, but most of the time not. It was a favorite snack when it was in season. Fresh chickpeas taste nothing like the dried variety, which tend to be nuttier and starchier. Eating fresh chickpeas is a little messy. You pop them in your mouth and eat the green pea inside. The majority of the flavors get soaked up in the pods.

6–8 SERVINGS

¼ cup (50 g) sea salt

1 lb (454 g) fresh chickpeas, in the pod

Canola oil

⅓ cup (91 ml) fresh lemon juice

Extra virgin olive oil, for garnish

Maldon salt, for garnish

Bring a large saucepot with about 4 quarts (3.8 L) of water to a boil, then add the salt. Blanch the chickpeas for about 2 minutes, or until the pods are slightly soft. Drain the water, and dry the chickpeas by patting them with a towel.

Heat a cast-iron pan over high heat until smoking; add a small film of canola oil. Working in batches, cook the chickpeas until they start to brown and blister, about 3 minutes. Shake the pan around and continue to cook on high heat until the chickpeas are evenly charred and slightly soft, shaking the pan often. Add the lemon juice and toss to combine. Remove from the heat and drizzle with a generous amount of olive oil and garnish with a sprinkling of crunchy salt. Serve immediately.

CHEF'S TIP: The fresh chickpeas can also be roasted in the oven. Just toss them with a little oil and sea salt and roast them at 400°F (205°C) until they start to brown, about 8–10 minutes.

Cucumber & Yogurt Salad with Dill, Sour Cherries and Rose Petals

I realize that the combination might seem odd, but trust me, it's delicious and addicting. This recipe is a riff on the Persian yogurt and cucumber dip. I swapped out the traditional raisins for dried sour cherries and the pedestrian walnuts for the more luxurious pistachios.

8 SERVINGS

2 garlic cloves, finely grated

2 cups (400 g) Homemade Thick Yogurt (page 189), or Greek yogurt

1 tsp (5 ml) fresh lemon juice

1 tbsp (4 g) fresh dill, roughly chopped

1½ tsp (0.8 g) dried mint

3 small Lebanese cucumbers, finely diced

Sea salt

½ cup (62 g) pistachios, crushed

1½ tsp (1.4 g) dried rose petals, crushed

3 tbsp (30 g) dried sour cherries, chopped

Fresh mint and dill leaves, for garnish

Extra virgin olive oil, for garnish

In a medium bowl, whisk together the garlic with the yogurt, lemon juice, dill and mint. Fold in the cucumbers and season with salt to taste. Spoon into a serving bowl and garnish with the pistachios, rose petals, dried cherries, mint and dill leaves. Drizzle with a generous amount of olive oil and serve immediately.

CHEF'S TIP: Can't find dried rose petals? No problem! Purchase some organic, non-sprayed roses and hang upside down in a dry, warm place until they are dry. These keep in an airtight container indefinitely. You can do the same with mint if you desire.

Fresh Chickpeas with Cumin Butter

The combination of chickpeas and cumin is classic, and for good reason: it works. Cumin finds its way into many chickpea-based Middle Eastern dishes, from hummus and falafel to chickpea stew; it's everywhere. In this simple recipe, the fresh chickpeas bathe in cumin-spiked butter, giving them a rich and earthy flavor profile.

6 SERVINGS

FOR THE CUMIN BUTTER

¼ lb (114 g) unsalted butter, at room temperature

1 tbsp (6 g) cumin seeds, toasted and ground

1 tsp (5 ml) fresh lemon juice

Sea salt

FOR THE CHICKPEAS

½ cup (100 g) sea salt

½ tsp (2.5 g) baking soda

2 lb (908 g) fresh chickpeas, in the pod

2 tbsp (8 g) flat-leaf parsley, coarsely chopped

FOR THE CUMIN BUTTER

Place all the ingredients in a small mixing bowl, season with salt and mix to combine. Place in an airtight container and refrigerate for up to 2 weeks or freeze for up to a month.

FOR THE CHICKPEAS

Bring a large pot with about 4 quarts (3.8 L) of water to a boil, then add the salt and baking soda. Blanch the chickpeas for about 3 minutes, or until the pod softens up and the chickpeas are softer. Shock the cooked chickpeas in a water bath of equal amounts of ice and water. Once cooled, drain and pick the chickpeas out of the pod, discarding the pods.

Place a large skillet over moderate heat. Add the shelled chickpeas with a few tablespoons (45 ml) of water, followed by the cumin butter; swirl the pan until the butter is melted and fully incorporated into the chickpeas. Garnish with the parsley and serve warm.

> **CHEF'S TIP:** Baking soda helps green vegetables keep a beautiful vibrant color after cooking, but it's not essential to the recipe.

Fresh Figs with Za'atar and Fresh Cheese

Every time I eat a perfectly ripe fig it reminds me of my childhood. Growing up, I had a fig tree across the street from my house in Jordan. I remember sitting up in the tree with my friends, picking and snacking on the ripe fruit. The success of this recipe is all in the hands of the figs; be sure to select ripe figs, because anything else will yield a less-than-stellar salad.

6 SERVINGS

¼ cup (6 g) chervil, leaves

¼ cup (5 g) wild or baby arugula leaves

¼ cup (5 g) upland cress leaves

2 tsp (10 ml) extra virgin olive oil, plus more for garnish

A squeeze of fresh lemon juice

Sea salt

12 medium ripe figs, at room temperature

¼ cup (85 g) Fresh Cheese (page 179)

Za'atar (page 202), for garnish

Aged balsamic vinegar (the good stuff), for garnish

Maldon salt

In a medium bowl, toss the herbs and greens with the olive oil and lemon juice and season with salt. Arrange the salad on a platter to form a circle. Cut the figs into rounds and wedges and place them around the greens. Dot the fresh cheese around the figs. Garnish with the za'atar, a drizzle of balsamic, some olive oil and a sprinkling of Maldon salt.

CHEF'S TIP: When buying figs, be sure to pick ones that are soft but not mushy. Ugly ones tend to be the best-tasting ones. They should also have a noticeably sweet aroma.

Fried Artichokes with Tahini "Tarator"

Here, the quintessential Mediterranean vegetable gets a quick braise in a lemon-scented broth and then a light fry. The accompaniment is a tahini sauce that has Turkish roots but is very popular in the Middle East. The sauce also works well with other fried or roasted vegetables and fried seafood.

4 SERVINGS

FOR THE TAHINI "TARATOR"

1 cup (230 g) tahini

1 tsp (4 g) Homemade Thick Yogurt (page 189), or Greek yogurt

½ cup (34 g) flat-leaf parsley, finely chopped

½ cup (34 g) cilantro, finely chopped

2 garlic cloves, finely grated

¼ cup (60 ml) fresh lemon juice

About ½ cup (120 ml) water

Sea salt

FOR THE FRIED ARTICHOKES

1 tbsp (15.6 g) citric acid or ¼ cup (60 ml) lemon juice

12 baby artichokes

Sea salt

1 fresh thyme sprig

1 fresh bay leaf

1 cup (240 ml) extra virgin olive oil

1 cup (240 ml) white wine, preferably sauvignon blanc

1 lemon, halved

Canola oil, for deep-frying

Cornstarch, as needed

Ground sumac, for garnish

Ground Aleppo chile, for garnish

FOR THE TAHINI "TARATOR"

In a small mixing bowl, combine all the ingredients, except the water, season with salt and stir with a spoon. Slowly add the water while stirring. The tahini will thicken and start to break, then it will magically loosen up as you add more water. The sauce should have the consistency of thick cream. Refrigerate for 10–15 minutes to let the flavors meld. Can be made up to 4 hours ahead.

FOR THE FRIED ARTICHOKES

In a large mixing bowl, whisk 4 cups (960 ml) of water with the citric acid or the lemon juice. Working with one artichoke at a time, pull off and discard the dark green outer leaf. Using a sharp paring knife or serrated knife, trim off about ¼ inch (6 mm) of the leaf tips, then peel and trim the end of the stem, reserving as much of it as possible. Halve the artichoke and scrape out the hairy choke.

Place the halved artichoke in the acidulated water. Repeat with the remaining artichokes.

Drain the artichokes and place in a medium saucepot, season liberally with salt and add the thyme, bay leaf, olive oil and white wine. Squeeze the lemon into the pot and add the lemon halves. Bring to a simmer over moderately high heat, then reduce the heat to low. Cover and simmer until the artichokes are tender when pierced with a fork, about 15–20 minutes. Let the artichokes cool in the cooking liquid for 30 minutes.

In a large, heavy pot no more than half filled with oil, or a deep fryer, heat the oil to 350°F (177°C). Meanwhile, drain and pat the artichokes dry with a paper towel. In a large bowl, toss a small amount of the artichokes liberally in cornstarch to coat, shake off the excess cornstarch and carefully place the artichokes in the oil and cook for 2–3 minutes, turning them over so they color evenly. Once lightly browned, use a slotted spoon to remove the artichokes from the oil and drain briefly on absorbent towels, seasoning with a small amount of salt and a sprinkling of sumac and Aleppo chile. Repeat with the remaining artichokes. Place the fried artichokes on a serving platter and serve with the tahini "tarator" on the side for dipping.

CHEF'S TIP: Reuse the poaching liquid a few more times, adding more white wine if necessary.

Fried Cauliflower with Sheep's Milk Feta Fondue and North African Spices

I love cauliflower. I grew up eating it in many different preparations, from fried to sautéed to pickled. I'm a fan. For this recipe, I thought, let's pack as much flavor into this fairly bland vegetable, so naturally I gravitated toward the pungent sheep's milk cheese and heady North African spices and herbs. When the regulars at Saffron heard that I was working on a book, the most commonly asked question was if the recipe for the fried cauliflower was going to be included. It is hands down the most popular menu item at the restaurant; eat your heart out, chicken! So without any further ado, here it is: the glorious fried cauliflower.

8 SERVINGS

FOR THE FETA FONDUE

6 oz (170 g) Bulgarian sheep's milk feta

FOR THE CAULIFLOWER

Sea salt

1 tsp (3.4 g) ground turmeric

2 tbsp (30 ml) fresh lemon juice

1 head (1½ lb [660 g]) cauliflower, halved, cored and cut into 1" (3 cm) florets

FOR THE BATTER

6 tbsp (48 g) cornstarch

1½ cups (205 g) cake flour

1 tsp (4.6 g) baking soda

½ tsp sea salt

3 tbsp (45 g) Sriracha

1½ cups (360 ml) soda water

FOR THE NORTH AFRICAN SPICE

3½ tbsp (21 g) cumin seeds, toasted and ground

1½ tbsp (9 g) Spanish sweet smoked paprika

½ tsp (3 g) citric acid

1 tsp (2 g) cayenne

1½ tsp (1.7 g) fresh dill, finely chopped

1½ tsp (2 g) cilantro, finely chopped

2 tbsp (22 g) kosher salt

TO FINISH

Canola oil

Sea salt

2 tbsp (8 g) flat-leaf parsley, finely chopped

2 tbsp (6.6 g) fresh dill, finely chopped

FOR THE FETA FONDUE

In a food processor, puree the feta until it becomes very smooth, scraping down the sides as necessary, about 5 minutes. It should have a pourable consistency similar to heavy cream. Add 1 teaspoon (5 ml) of the feta brine or water if the fondue is too thick.

FOR THE CAULIFLOWER

Bring a large saucepot with about 12 cups (2.8 L) of water to a boil. Season liberally with salt, then add the turmeric and lemon juice. Cook the cauliflower in the boiling water until it starts to become tender, about 2–4 minutes. Set a large colander in the sink, drain the cauliflower and discard the poaching liquid. Cool the cauliflower on a parchment-lined baking sheet in the refrigerator.

FOR THE BATTER

In a large mixing bowl, combine all of the dry ingredients and whisk to combine. Add the Sriracha and soda water, and whisk until combined. The batter should have the consistency of honey; add an extra 1 tablespoon (15 ml) of soda water if needed.

FOR THE NORTH AFRICAN SPICE

In small mixing bowl, mix all the ingredients thoroughly. Place on a parchment-lined baking sheet and let dry overnight in a cool place. Place in an airtight container and store for up to 2 weeks.

TO FINISH

Fill a large, heavy pot (or a deep fryer) no more than halfway with oil and heat the oil to 350°F (177°C). Working in 3–4 batches, dip the cauliflower in the batter, shake off excess batter and carefully drop in the oil; cook for 3–5 minutes, stirring occasionally, until they are golden brown. Use a slotted spoon to remove the cauliflower from the oil, place in a large mixing bowl and season with a liberal amount of the North African spice, salt, parsley and dill. Repeat with the remaining cauliflower and serve with the feta fondue on the side for dipping.

CHEF'S TIP: You must use a very soft feta with higher water content for this recipe. A French or an Egyptian feta may also be used.

Fried Stuffed Olives with Capers, Anchovy and Haloumi

To me, olives are a prefect way to wake up the palate, and this recipe is packed with flavor that is guaranteed to do just that. The salty and briny elements of the olives, capers, anchovies and haloumi are balanced with the heat from the chile flakes and the freshness of the parsley and lemon. Pair them with the Roasted Lemonade (page 170) for a perfect pre-dinner snack.

4–8 SERVINGS

12 good-quality anchovy fillets in oil, rinsed and roughly chopped

1 tbsp (8.6 g) brined capers, drained and rinsed

1 tbsp (4 g) flat-leaf parsley, finely chopped

½ tsp (0.7 g) chile flakes

1 garlic clove, finely grated

¼ cup (30 g) grated haloumi cheese

¼ cup (62 g) ricotta

Zest and juice of ½ lemon

24–30 large green olives, pitted

Canola oil, for frying

½ cup (63 g) all-purpose flour

2 eggs, beaten

1 cup (110 g) fresh breadcrumbs, finely buzzed in a food processor

Lemon wedges, for serving

Place the anchovies, capers, parsley, chile flakes and garlic in a food processor and pulse until chunky; scrape down the sides of the bowl, add the haloumi, ricotta, lemon zest and juice and pulse to combine. The mixture should be a little chunky, but homogenous. Place the mixture in a disposable piping bag and stuff the olives, making sure not to overfill.

Meanwhile, fill a large, heavy pot (or a deep fryer) no more than halfway with oil and heat the oil to 350°F (177°C).

In 3 separate small bowls, place the flour, eggs and breadcrumbs. Dredge the olives in the flour. Using a slotted spoon, remove the olives and place in the bowl with the beaten egg. Coat the olives with the egg and then transfer to the bowl of breadcrumbs and coat.

Carefully place the olives in the oil and cook for 2–3 minutes, until they are golden. Use a slotted spoon to remove the olives from the oil and drain briefly on absorbent towels. Repeat with the remaining olives. Serve with the lemon wedges.

CHEF'S TIP: I like to use the Sicilian Castelvetvano olives. These intense, bright green olives are not cured in the traditional way, which helps keep their bright green color and sweet flavor.

Grandma's Slow-Cooked Green Beans

The idea of green beans cooked for hours will probably make most classic French chefs' heads explode. The beans are cooked with dark spices, tomato, garlic and lots of olive oil for about 2 hours, until they start to fall apart, a cooking method that is popular in the eastern Mediterranean. This recipe is actually adapted from a recipe that I found in the cookbook that my mother, father and uncle wrote in the late 1980s. I was so moved by the simplicity and depth of flavor in the recipe that it inspired me to "overhaul" the menu at Saffron. At a time when young chefs were trying to be groundbreaking and avant-garde, I looked at a humble plate of "overcooked" green beans as the inspiration to showcase the bold flavors of my heritage. I like to squeeze a little lemon and scoop it with warm pita bread, sopping up all the delicious cooking juices.

8 SERVINGS

1 cup (240 ml) extra virgin olive oil

1 small yellow onion, thinly sliced

Sea salt

3 lb (1.4 kg) fresh green beans, trimmed

1 tbsp (8.4 g) Se7en Spice (page 184)

1 tsp (2.7 g) paprika

2 cups (500 g) San Marzano tomatoes, crushed by hand

A pinch of chile flakes

3 garlic cloves, finely grated

Lemon wedges, to serve

Fresh pocket bread (pita), to serve

Heat the olive oil in a large, heavy-bottomed pot over moderate heat. Add the onion, season with salt and cook until translucent, about 5–8 minutes. Add the beans and cook for 5 minutes, stirring often. Add the se7en spice and paprika, season with salt and cook for 30 seconds to toast the spices. Add the tomatoes and stir to combine. Reduce the heat to low, cover and cook for 1½–2 hours, stirring often. The beans should start to melt and turn a dark shade of green, almost brown. If they still hold their texture and color, they are not done. Add a pinch of chile flakes, the garlic and season with more salt and se7en spice if needed. The finished product should have a pronounced spice level and a little raw garlic kick. Remove from the heat and let the flavors meld for a few hours, then refrigerate until ready to eat. Remove the beans from the refrigerator, place on a serving platter and bring to room temperature. Serve with lemon wedges and warmed pocket bread.

CHEF'S TIP: Because this will be served cold or at room temperature, be sure to season with salt a little heavier than you usually would, as food that is chilled tends to mute the salt.

Grilled Beef Lettuce Wraps with Tabbouleh

In the Middle East, everyone has strong opinions about what version of a dish is most authentic or better. I feel that tabbouleh is one of those that evokes very different ideas. The one thing that most will agree upon is that tabbouleh is a parsley salad with a little bulgur. I won't even attempt to try to talk about the recipes that include cucumbers, as I fear for my life.

4 SERVINGS AS AN APPETIZER, 2 AS A LIGHT MEAL

FOR THE STEAK

2 (12 oz [340 g]) pieces of beef strip loin or rib eye

1 tbsp (15 ml) canola oil

Sea salt

Fresh ground black pepper

FOR THE TABBOULEH

2 tbsp (19 g) fine bulgur wheat

2 cups (135 g) flat-leaf parsley, finely chopped

¼ cup (45 g) finely chopped fresh tomato

1 green onion, thinly sliced

3 tbsp (4.8 g) fresh mint, torn

2 tbsp (30 ml) fresh lemon juice

3 tbsp (45 ml) extra virgin olive oil

Sea salt

Fresh ground black pepper

TO SERVE

1 head Bibb lettuce, leaves separated

3 small radishes, thinly sliced

FOR THE STEAK

Preheat the gas, charcoal grill or grill pan to moderate-high heat.

Bring the steaks to room temperature. Brush with canola oil and season liberally with sea salt and black pepper. Grill the steaks until firm and charred on the outside, about 2–5 minutes per side, depending on their thickness and how you like the meat done. Place the steaks on a cutting board; rest the meat for 5 minutes. Slice the steaks crosswise into ½" (13 mm)-thick slices.

FOR THE TABBOULEH

Place the bulgur in a fine-mesh strainer, rinse under running water and rub with your fingertips until the water starts to run clear. Drain the water and place in a medium mixing bowl and let stand for 10–15 minutes. With a fork, fluff and break up the bulgur; it should have softened by this time. If it doesn't, add a few drops of water or tomato juice from cutting the tomatoes. Mix the remaining ingredients with the bulgur, then season with salt and a liberal dose of black pepper. The final product should be a little spicy from the black pepper with a balanced acidity.

TO SERVE

Arrange the lettuce leaves on a large platter or individual plates. Spoon tabbouleh in the center of the lettuce, top with the beef and sliced radishes and serve immediately.

CHEF'S TIP: As you will notice here, the bulgur is not cooked. In my opinion, fine bulgur doesn't need to be cooked; it absorbs enough liquid by being rinsed or soaked for a few minutes. To impart more flavor, you can soak it in lemon juice or some of the tomato juice drippings from cutting the tomatoes.

Haloumi with Black Figs, Ouzo and Black Pepper

Haloumi is a sheep's milk cheese from Cyprus that is popular in the Middle East. Here it's served with poached black figs that are flavored with the anise liqueur ouzo and cracked black peppercorns to balance the sweetness of the figs. Anise is one of the world's oldest cultivated spices. The sweet licorice flavor is used in a great range of alcoholic beverages around the Mediterranean, from ouzo to pernod, raki and arak. Any of these spirits can be substituted in the recipe. The poached figs are a great accompaniment to any cheese plate as well.

5–10 SERVINGS

FOR THE POACHED FIGS

16 dried Black Mission figs, stems trimmed and halved lengthwise

1 cup (240 ml) water

½ cup (100 g) sugar

1 tsp (2 g) anise seeds, lightly crushed

½ tsp (1.3 g) black peppercorns, toasted and coarsely ground or cracked

¼ cup (60 ml) ouzo

FOR THE HALOUMI

Canola oil, for cooking

2 (7-10 oz [198-284 g]) packages haloumi cheese, cut into ½" (13 mm) pieces

Extra virgin olive oil, for garnish

Dill leaves, for garnish

FOR THE POACHED FIGS

In a medium saucepan, combine the figs, water and sugar and bring to a boil. Add the anise seeds and black pepper. Cover and simmer over moderate heat for 15 minutes. Uncover and simmer until the liquid reduces into a glaze, and the figs are tender but not mushy, about 15 minutes, adding the ouzo in the last 5 minutes of cooking. Let cool completely in the syrup. The poached figs can be refrigerated for up to 1 month. Serve at room temperature.

FOR THE HALOUMI

Heat a thin layer of canola oil in a large nonstick skillet over high heat. Add the haloumi and cook undisturbed for 1 minute, until it is a deep golden brown. Flip and cook for 30 seconds.

Place on a serving platter and garnish with the poached figs and some of the fig poaching liquid. Finish with a drizzle of olive oil and a few leaves of dill.

CHEF'S TIP: You can make a fig jam by simply pulsing the figs in a food processor along with any remaining poaching liquid.

Classic Hummus

I was on the fence about including a recipe for hummus in this book; after all, it's everywhere—from grocery stores and restaurants to schools and airports. I have a love/hate relationship with this stuff. I love the taste and the process of making it, but I don't love that it is one of the first things that people associate with Arabic food. After long deliberation, here it is: the hummus recipe that I've adapted from the cookbook that my father, mother and uncle started to write but never finished. Hummus styles reflect personal preferences in the Middle East. Some like it a little chunky with lots of cumin; others, smooth with a little nudge of fresh chile ... you get the picture. This recipe yields an ultra-smooth hummus that has a heavier tahini ratio than most hummus recipes, which makes for a richer hummus. Although the chickpeas require some advance preparation, once you have them cooked, making the hummus is a breeze. Just do yourself a favor and don't use canned chickpeas, as they won't break down as well as the freshly cooked ones when pureed. They also have a distinct tinny flavor that will alter the recipe drastically. Serve with warm pita bread or crudités.

4–6 SERVINGS

1½ cups (300 g) dried chickpeas, soaked in water overnight

½ tsp (2.3 g) baking soda

Sea salt

2 garlic cloves, finely grated

2-3 tsp (10-15 ml) fresh lemon juice

1¼–1½ cups (280-336 g) tahini

4 tbsp (60 ml) extra virgin olive oil, plus more for garnish

Paprika, for garnish

Cumin seeds, toasted and ground, for garnish, optional

Drain the soaked chickpeas and place in a medium saucepan and cover with cold water, about 2 inches (5 cm) over the chickpeas. Add the baking soda and cook over moderate-high heat until they become soft and start to break down, about 1-1½ hours. Season the chickpeas with salt and cool them down in the cooking liquid.

Once completely chilled, place the chickpeas, along with ¼ cup (60 ml) of the reserved cooking liquid, garlic and lemon juice in a food processor. Puree until very smooth while occasionally scraping down the sides of the machine, about 4 minutes. Add the tahini and the olive oil and continue to process until the hummus thickens. Adjust the seasoning with more lemon and salt, if desired.

Spoon the hummus into a bowl or plate and garnish with paprika, cumin and a generous amount of olive oil.

CHEF'S TIP: Adding the baking soda to the chickpeas while they cook helps them break down and become soft, which helps in making the hummus into a very smooth puree. The cooked chickpeas can be frozen for up to a month in an airtight freezer bag. Just thaw under running water.

Hummus Royale
with Spiced Beef and Pine Nuts

I love the contrast of the ultra-smooth hummus with the spiced beef and pine nuts. Many different variations of spiced meat and hummus are seen all over the Levant. Some chop the meat by hand into smaller chunks, which I sometimes prefer to the ground meat. Lamb also works well in place of the beef. Serve with warm pita bread or crudités.

4–6 SERVINGS

1 ½ tbsp (21 g) Clarified Butter (page 203), ghee or canola oil

2 tbsp (16 g) pine nuts

½ small yellow onion, finely diced

Sea salt

¼ lb (113 g) chopped sirloin or coarse ground beef, preferably freshly ground chuck from a butcher

1 tsp (2.8 g) Se7en Spice (page 184)

Classic Hummus (page 40)

1 tbsp (4 g) flat-leaf parsley, coarsely chopped

Paprika, for garnish

Extra virgin olive oil, for garnish

Heat the clarified butter in a medium skillet over moderate heat. Add the pine nuts and cook, stirring continually, until golden, about 2 minutes. Use a slotted spoon to remove them from the pan, add the onion, season with salt and cook until the onion becomes translucent, stirring often, about 3 minutes. Add the meat and season with Se7en Spice and salt. Cook over moderately high heat until browned and barely cooked through, about 2–4 minutes. If using the ground meat, break it up with a wooden spoon and cook on moderately high heat until browned and cooked through, about 5 minutes.

Spoon the hummus into a shallow bowl; make a deep well in the center. Spoon the spiced meat into the middle and garnish with the toasted pine nuts, parsley, paprika and a generous amount of olive oil.

Hummus with Caramelized Paprika Butter and Za'atar

Hummus purists are probably wagging their fingers at me. The addition of the caramelized paprika butter is loosely inspired by a Turkish-style hummus that substitutes butter for the tahini and serves it warm. Rather than changing the recipe, I just topped the classic hummus with the caramelized paprika butter and added za'atar. Make sure that the hummus is at room temperature before adding the butter, as the butter will harden up as it sits. The caramelized paprika butter adds smoky and nutty notes to the hummus, while the za'atar adds an herbaceous flavor. Serve with warm pita bread or crudités.

4–6 SERVINGS

Classic Hummus (page 40)

Za'atar (page 202), for garnish

Caramelized Paprika Butter (page 176), as needed, warmed, for garnish

Follow the directions for the classic hummus. Spoon the hummus into a bowl, and with the back of a spoon make a slight hollow in the center. Garnish the edges of the hummus with za'atar and spoon the butter into the center of the bowl.

Kofta Meatballs with Pomegranate & Tahini

When I was growing up, making kofta was mainly my father's job. He enjoyed grilling skewers on a little charcoal grill on the rooftop. The smell of the meat drippings hitting the coals would fill the entire neighborhood, a smoke signal, if you will, for me to come home. This recipe is inspired by the flavor of my father's kofta, with a few artistic liberties.

6–10 SERVINGS, ABOUT 40 MEATBALLS

FOR THE KOFTA MEATBALLS

1 lb (454 g) ground lamb, preferably from shoulder

1 lb (454 g) ground beef, preferably chuck with 20% fat

1½ tbsp (12.6 g) Se7en Spice (page 184)

1 tbsp (8.4 g) Garam Masala (page 181)

1 tsp (2.7 g) Spanish sweet smoked paprika

1 tsp (1.4 g) chile flakes

½ small onion, finely grated

4 garlic cloves, finely grated

½ cup (34 g) flat-leaf parsley, finely chopped

½ cup (34 g) cilantro, finely chopped

Sea salt

TO FINISH

4 tbsp (56 g) unsalted butter

½ cup (67 g) pine nuts

1½ cups (360 ml) chicken stock

¼ cup (60 ml) pomegranate molasses

Tahini Sauce (page 175), as needed

Seeds of 1 medium pomegranate

¼ cup (17 g) flat-leaf parsley, coarsely chopped

FOR THE KOFTA MEATBALLS

In a bowl, combine all of the kofta ingredients, season with salt and mix together with your hands, making sure not to overmix. Form into 1 inch (3 cm) meatballs and press the mixture to ensure that each ball is tight and keeps its shape. Arrange on a parchment-lined baking sheet and refrigerate until you are ready to cook them, up to 24 hours.

Preheat the oven to 400°F (205°C). Bake the kofta meatballs until they start to brown and are almost cooked through, about 4–6 minutes.

TO FINISH

In a large frying pan, melt the butter and allow it to brown lightly; add the pine nuts and cook for 2 minutes, stirring often. Add the meatballs and stock to the frying pan and simmer until the stock is almost evaporated and the meatballs are hot and cooked through, about 5–8 minutes. Drizzle in the pomegranate molasses and toss gently to coat the meatballs with the sauce. Place the meatballs in a serving bowl; drizzle with the tahini sauce and garnish with the pomegranate seeds and parsley.

CHEF'S TIP: The kofta could be formed into skewers, grilled over charcoal and served with some fresh pita.

Marinated Peppers with Toasted Garlic & Smoked Paprika

Here is a simple recipe of roasted and marinated peppers that makes an excellent mezze or can be served alongside meat or seafood. Serve with crusty bread to dip in the paprika-rich marinade.

8 SERVINGS

2 yellow bell peppers

2 red bell peppers

Extra virgin olive oil

Smoked Paprika & Toasted Garlic Vinaigrette (page 201)

Sea salt

2 tbsp (8 g) flat-leaf parsley, roughly chopped

Maldon salt

Preheat the oven to broil. Rub the bell peppers with olive oil and arrange them on a baking sheet. Broil the peppers for about 10–15 minutes, turning occasionally, until they are blistered and softened. Transfer the roasted peppers to a medium bowl, cover with plastic wrap and let cool completely. Peel and seed the cooled peppers and pat them dry. Cut the peppers into quarters and transfer them to a medium bowl. Add the dressing and toss to coat completely. Season with salt and let the peppers stand at room temperature for at least 1 hour and up to overnight.

To serve, place the marinated peppers on a large platter, drizzle some of the vinaigrette on top and garnish with the parsley and crunchy salt.

CHEF'S TIP: I prefer to use a gas range with exposed burners to roast the peppers. I do so by placing the peppers directly in the flame, turning them often until they are blistered.

Middle Eastern Sausage with Lemon & Pomegranate Molasses

The distinct sweet and tart flavor of the pomegranate molasses added to these little sausages is a signature Lebanese preparation. You can use Mirqaz Sausage (page 57) in place of the Na'anik for a spicy version.

4–6 SERVINGS

Canola oil

12 Middle Eastern Sausage (Na'anik) links (page 193)

¼ cup (34 g) pine nuts

¼ cup (60 ml) fresh lemon juice

1 tbsp (4 g) flat-leaf parsley, roughly chopped

Pomegranate molasses, for garnish

Fresh pocket bread (pita), for serving

Heat a small film of canola oil in a large frying pan and cook the sausages, undisturbed, for 2 minutes per side, over moderate-high heat. Lower the heat to medium and add the pine nuts; toast in the pan for 1 minute, stirring often. Add the lemon juice, and swirl the pan to combine the juice with the fat. Transfer to a serving platter. Garnish with the parsley and a drizzle of pomegranate molasses. Serve with fresh pocket bread.

Oysters with Pickled Coriander

Pickled coriander is one of my favorite condiments. The pickling softens the coriander seeds so they pop when you chew them. It also tames the flavors down. But the true star is the pickling liquid, which has a floral aroma and slight toasty, earthy notes. For this recipe, the pickled coriander is mixed with raw shallots to make a mignonette, a condiment that is typically served with raw oysters.

2–8 SERVINGS, DEPENDING ON YOUR COMPANY

FOR THE PICKLED CORIANDER MIGNONETTE

½ cup (32 g) coriander seeds

1 cup (240 ml) champagne vinegar

1 tsp (4 g) sugar

1 tsp (2.8 g) sea salt

1 large shallot, finely minced

FOR THE OYSTERS

2 dozen ultra-fresh oysters, shucked

Micro cilantro or very small leaves of cilantro, for garnish

Fruity extra virgin olive oil, for garnish

FOR THE PICKLED CORIANDER MIGNONETTE

In a small pot over moderate heat, toast the coriander until fragrant, about 30 seconds, while constantly swirling the pan to keep the coriander from burning. Remove from the heat and allow to cool slightly. Add the vinegar, sugar and salt, then return to the heat and bring to a boil. Remove from the heat and refrigerate the pickled coriander for up to a month in an airtight container.

When ready to use, combine the pickled coriander with the shallot in a small mixing bowl and season with salt.

FOR THE OYSTERS

Arrange the oysters on a platter and top each with about ½ teaspoon of the mignonette, making sure to get some of the coriander seeds. Garnish with the cilantro and a few drops of olive oil. Serve immediately.

Paella Croquettes with Saffron Aioli

The Arabs introduced rice to the Spaniards, and it is the base of this iconic paella dish. Once a poor man's dish, even the name, paella, is believed to have originated from the *baqiya*, which means "leftovers" in Arabic. This recipe is not authentic, but it is delicious, turning this dish into a perfect snack.

8–12 SERVINGS

FOR THE PAELLA CROQUETTES

4 tbsp (56 g) unsalted butter

1 small onion, finely diced

½ cup (68 g) garlic cloves, thinly sliced

Sea salt

1½ cups (280 g) short-grain rice (Calasparra, Bomba or Arborio)

1 tsp (0.9 g) saffron threads, crushed with fingertips

½ tsp (1.3 g) Spanish sweet smoked paprika

Pinch of chile flakes

8 piquillo peppers, cut into ¼" (6 mm) dice

½ cup (120 ml) dry white wine

1 cup (250 g) tomato puree, preferably San Marzano

3½ cups (840 ml) Lobster Stock (page 192) or chicken stock, warmed

8 oz (227 g) rock shrimp, cut into ¼" (6 mm) pieces (may substitute other small shrimp)

1 cup (134 g) frozen peas, thawed

1 tbsp (4 g) flat-leaf parsley, finely chopped

¼ cup (25 g) finely grated Parmigianino-Reggiano cheese

½ cup (62.5 g) all-purpose flour, for dusting

2 eggs, beaten with 1 tbsp (15 ml) milk

1½ cups (96 g) panko breadcrumbs, finely buzzed in food processor

Canola oil, for frying

2 lemons, cut into wedges, for garnish

FOR THE SAFFRON AIOLI

3 tbsp (45 ml) Saffron Water "Tea" (page 199)

2 egg yolks

2 garlic cloves, finely grated

2 tbsp (30 ml) fresh lemon juice

Sea salt

Pinch of cayenne

1½ cups (353 ml) neutral oil (grapeseed, canola or soybean oil)

FOR THE PAELLA CROQUETTES

In a large saucepan, melt the butter. Add the onion and garlic, season with salt and cook over low heat, stirring often, until the onions are translucent and softened, about 8 minutes. Add the rice and cook, stirring often, until well coated with butter. Stir in the saffron, paprika and chile flakes and cook for 1 minute, stirring continuously, to bring out the flavor of the spices. Add the piquillo peppers and white wine; cook, stirring constantly, until the wine is absorbed, about 2 minutes. Add the tomato puree and the warm stock, ½ cup (120 ml) at a time, and cook, stirring constantly between additions, until the liquid is absorbed. The rice is done when it's slightly soft, about 25–30 minutes total. Stir in the shrimp and continue to cook for 1 minute, following with the peas, parsley and grated cheese. Transfer to a parchment-lined baking sheet and let cool.

Line another large baking sheet with parchment. Put the flour, egg wash and breadcrumbs in three separate shallow bowls. Using lightly moistened hands or a small ice cream scoop, shape the rice mixture into 24 equal-size balls, rolling them between your hands. Transfer the rice balls to the baking sheet. Dust the rice balls with flour, tapping off the excess. Dip them in the egg wash, remove them with a fork, let the excess egg wash drip back into the bowl and then roll in the breadcrumbs.

In a large, heavy pot (or a deep fryer), no more than half filled with oil, heat the oil to 350°F (177°C). Working in batches, carefully lower the croquettes into the oil and fry until golden brown, turning occasionally, about 5–7 minutes. Remove from the oil and drain briefly on absorbent towels. Season with a small amount of salt and a squeeze of fresh lemon juice. Serve immediately with the saffron aioli on the side.

FOR THE SAFFRON AIOLI

In a blender or food processor, combine the saffron water, egg yolks, garlic and lemon juice. Season with salt and a pinch of cayenne. Whirl on moderate speed until the mixture becomes bubbly, about 1 minute. Turn the speed down to low and gradually add the oil in a steady, thin stream, until very thick and creamy. Season with more salt if needed.

CHEF'S TIP: A traditional paella is cooked in a *paellera*, a wide, round and shallow pan that helps ensure that the rice cooks in a thin layer to achieve a crusty bottom layer. You can use this recipe as a guideline for making paella. Omit the cheese and after adding the liquid, don't stir the rice as much.

Smoky Eggplant Dip with Charmoula

In this North African variation on the classic baba ganoush, the addition of the charmoula adds layers of flavor to the luscious puree. Charring eggplant is a trick that Middle Eastern cooks have in their arsenal; it imparts a unique flavor that is the essence of the old world cuisine. If you omit the charmoula, add a small amount of chopped hot peppers and double the amount of lemon juice; you will have classic baba ganoush.

8–10 SERVINGS

3 large eggplants

½ cup (118 g) Charmoula (page 177)

3 tbsp (45 ml) fresh lemon juice

3 tbsp (45 ml) extra virgin olive oil, plus more for garnish

1 cup (230 g) tahini

Sea salt

1 tbsp (4 g) cilantro, roughly chopped

Spanish sweet smoked paprika, for garnish

Heat a gas or charcoal grill to moderate-high heat. Prick the eggplant with a fork 4–6 times, place on the grill and cook until the skin is heavily charred, almost burnt, and the flesh is soft, 15–20 minutes, turning them occasionally. Place the eggplant in a plastic container and cover for 5 minutes, allowing the eggplant to steam. Once cool enough to handle, split the eggplant down the middle lengthwise and scoop out the flesh, being careful not to get any black bits from the skin. Roughly chop and then drain the flesh in a fine-mesh colander for about 1 hour to remove as much of the water as possible.

Place the eggplant pulp in a medium bowl, combine with the charmoula, lemon juice, olive oil and tahini, season with salt and let the flavors meld for at least an hour. Spoon the eggplant onto a serving platter or bowl; garnish with the cilantro, a dusting of paprika and a drizzle of olive oil.

CHEF'S TIP: If you don't have access to a charcoal or gas grill, you can achieve similar results by using a gas range with exposed burners and placing the eggplant directly on the flame.

Feta Flan with Tomatoes and Black Olives

The feta flan is a luxurious centerpiece to this Greek-salad-inspired appetizer. Using sheep's milk feta helps keep the flan light and creamy. I would not suggest using a cow's milk feta, as the texture of the flan will be denser. In the wintertime, when tomatoes are out of season, I like substituting Roasted Tomatoes (page 204).

12 SERVINGS

FOR THE FETA FLAN

8 oz (227 g) cream cheese, cubed, at room temperature

3 oz (85 g) sheep's milk feta, cubed, at room temperature

1 egg

½ cup (120 ml) heavy cream

FOR THE RED WINE & THYME VINAIGRETTE

1 small shallot, finely chopped

1 garlic clove, finely chopped

1½ tbsp (23 ml) good-quality red wine vinegar

1 tbsp (2 g) fresh thyme leaves

3 tbsp (45 ml) extra virgin olive oil

Sea salt

FOR THE TOMATO SALAD

4 cups (750 g) cherry tomatoes in assorted colors, large ones cut in half

½ cup (94 g) kalamata olives, pitted

Thyme leaves, for garnish

Maldon salt

FOR THE FETA FLAN

Preheat the oven to 325°F (163°C).

In a mixer fitted with a whip attachment, combine the cream cheese and feta and mix on medium-high speed until completely soft and there are no lumps of cheese. Add the egg and whip for 30 seconds. Add the cream mix on medium speed until well incorporated, about 1 minute.

Spray twelve 4-ounce (118 ml) silicone flexi molds or disposable aluminum foil custard cups with cooking spray. Pour the flan batter into the prepared molds and carefully tap the molds on the countertop a few times to remove excess air bubbles. Set the molds in a small roasting pan and pour enough hot water into the pan to reach halfway up the side of each mold. Transfer the pan to the oven and bake for about 30–40 minutes, until the batter is just set and no longer jiggly. Remove the pan from the oven and let cool to room temperature. Remove the molds from the pan and freeze for at least 3 hours, preferably overnight. Remove the frozen flan by gently popping it out of each mold. Thaw for 2 hours at room temperature before serving.

FOR THE RED WINE & THYME VINAIGRETTE

In a small bowl, whisk all the ingredients and season with salt. Reserve.

FOR THE TOMATO SALAD

In a medium bowl, combine the tomatoes and olives, drizzle with a small amount of the vinaigrette and toss gently to combine. Carefully place the thawed feta flans in the center of individual plates. Place the tomato salad around the flan and garnish with thyme leaves and a sprinkling of crunchy salt.

Mirqaz Sausage Stew with Baked Eggs

This is a comfort dish for me. I like it as a hearty breakfast or lunch. The recipes for mirqaz and the tomato sauce make more than what you will need for a serving. I like to make extra sauce and freeze it in plastic bags for when I'm in a hurry and craving this dish. The mirqaz can be made into links or just left loose. Either way, it can be frozen for up to a month. So, if you have eggs, you should be able to whip this up in no time. Serve with a crusty loaf of bread.

6 SERVINGS

FOR THE MIRQAZ SAUSAGE

5 lb (2.3 kg) ground lamb, preferably from shoulder

8 oz (227 g) tomato paste

6 oz (170 g) Harissa (page 185)

3 tbsp (22.5 g) caraway seeds, toasted and ground

3 tbsp (25 g) sea salt

20 feet (6 m) sheep casings, optional

FOR THE TOMATO SAUCE

2 tbsp (30 ml) canola oil

2 large red peppers, cut into ¼" (6 mm) dice

½ small onion, finely diced

8 garlic cloves, thinly sliced

Sea salt

4 cups (1 kg) San Marzano tomatoes, crushed by hand

1 tsp (4 g) sugar

2 cups (328 g) Cooked Chickpeas (page 204)

3-4 tbsp (34-48 g) Harissa (page 185)

TO FINISH

Canola oil, for panfrying

6 eggs

¼ cup (10 g) cilantro, coarsely chopped

FOR THE MIRQAZ SAUSAGE

In a large mixing bowl or a stand mixer fitted with the paddle attachment, combine all of the ingredients, except the sheep casings, and knead or beat until well combined and a sticky mass forms, about 1 minute; be careful not to let the meat get too warm or overmix. Refrigerate for 2 hours and up to overnight.

If using the sheep casings, soak in warm water for 30 minutes. Drain and rinse the casings. Place the sausage stuffer (but not the stuffer tube) in the freezer for 15 minutes. Set up the sausage stuffer, lightly oil the stuffer tube and attach it to the stuffer. Slide the end of the casing onto the tube and push it back gently, adding more and more of the casing to cover the length of the tube, leaving 2 inches (5 cm) at the end. Tightly pack the sausage mixture into the stuffing canister. Crank the sausage stuffer very slowly until the meat emerges from the tube and tie a knot at the trailing end of the casing. Slowly crank the sausage into the casing, making sure not to overstuff the casing—you want thin, uniform sausages for even cooking. Once you have filled the casing, tie off the other end and twist the casing to create twelve 4-6 inch (10-15 cm) long links. Repeat with the remaining sausage and casing. Refrigerate, uncovered, overnight.

FOR THE TOMATO SAUCE

Meanwhile, heat the oil in a large saucepan over moderate heat and add the peppers, onion and garlic, and season with salt. Stir and cook over moderate heat until the peppers are softened and onions are translucent, about 5-7 minutes. Add the crushed tomatoes, bring to a gentle simmer and continue to cook for 10-15 minutes, or until the sauce is thickened. Finish with the sugar, chickpeas and harissa, and season with salt.

TO FINISH

Preheat the oven to 350°F (177°C). Cut the 12 sausages into links. Heat a small film of canola oil in a large ovenproof frying pan and cook the sausages for 5 minutes over moderate-high heat, moving them often. Pour a ½" (13 mm) layer of the tomato sauce over the sausages. Make 6 little dips in the sauce and crack the eggs into the dips. Use a fork to swirl the egg whites a little with the sauce, making sure not to break the yolks. Bake for 7-9 minutes, until the egg whites are set but the yolks are still runny. Remove from oven, garnish with the cilantro.

> **CHEF'S TIP:** Be sure to keep all of your equipment and ingredients very cold when making sausage, as the fat will start to melt and make for a not-so-sexy sausage.

Goat Cheese & Date Tart with Caramelized Onions and Thyme

This recipe is one of my favorite uses of soft goat cheese. Medjool dates are large, sweet dates that pair perfectly with the goat cheese. The pastry is a very simple, all-purpose dough that you will keep in your arsenal for years to come. I love serving this with simple roasted duck breast, or on its own as a vegetarian entrée or starter. The accompanying frisee salad is a crucial element; otherwise, I feel that the tart is too sweet and rich.

8 INDIVIDUAL TARTS

FOR THE TART DOUGH

2 cups (250 g) all-purpose flour, plus more for dusting

1 tsp (2.8 g) sea salt

½ lb (224 g) unsalted butter, cubed, well chilled

½ lb (224 g) cream cheese, cubed, well chilled

FOR THE CARAMELIZED ONIONS

1 tbsp (15 ml) canola oil

2 lb (907 g) sweet onions, thinly sliced

Sea salt

2 tbsp (30 ml) sweet oloroso sherry or water

Freshly ground black pepper

TO FINISH

½ lb (228 g) soft goat cheese

4 medjool dates, pitted and cut into slivers

1 tbsp (2 g) fresh thyme leaves, picked

2 medium heads frisee, green tips and thick, white bottom parts trimmed

Red Wine & Thyme Vinaigrette (page 56), as needed

Sea salt

Freshly ground black pepper

Garam Masala (page 181), for garnish

FOR THE TART DOUGH

In a mixer fitted with a paddle attachment, combine the flour and salt and mix on low, slowly adding the butter and cream cheese in small batches until the dough just forms a ball. Turn the dough out onto a lightly floured surface and pat it into a rectangle, then fold into thirds. Wrap the dough in plastic and refrigerate for at least 30 minutes or up to overnight.

Preheat the oven to 400°F (205°C). Remove the dough from the plastic wrap and place on a lightly floured surface. Roll out the chilled pastry to ¼ inch (6 mm) thick. Using a 5 inch (13 cm) round pastry cutter, cut out 8 rounds. Then carefully transfer the pastry rounds to a parchment-lined large baking sheet. Prick the middle of the dough with the tip of a fork and freeze until well chilled. Bake in the center of the oven for 10–15 minutes, until the tarts are lightly golden. Remove from the heat and let cool completely. Store in an airtight container for up to 2 days.

FOR THE CARAMELIZED ONIONS

In a skillet, heat the canola oil. Add the onions, season with salt and cook over moderately high heat until softened, about 8 minutes. Reduce the heat to moderately low and cook until the onions are melted and dark golden, about 20–25 minutes, stirring frequently. Add the sherry, scrape the bottom of the pan to remove any brown bits, and continue to cook until the liquid is evaporated and the onions are deep mahogany. Remove from the heat and season with salt and pepper. This can be done up to 2 days in advance.

TO FINISH

Preheat the oven to 400°F (205°C). On a parchment-lined baking sheet, spread half the goat cheese on top of the par-baked tarts. Divide the caramelized onions equally among the tarts, top with the medjool dates, then the remaining goat cheese and thyme leaves. Bake in the center of the oven for 5–7 minutes, until the goat cheese starts to brown and the tart is warmed.

In a medium bowl, toss the frisee with the vinaigrette and season with salt and pepper. Transfer the tarts to individual plates and garnish with a small frisee salad and a sprinkling of garam masala.

Grilled Prawns with Harissa

I love grilled prawns. Here they are marinated in a spicy harissa-laced marinade before a quick char on the grill. When I'm craving something spicier, I serve a little bowl of harissa mixed with olive oil on the side for dipping the prawns. You can substitute charmoula (page 177) for the harissa and get equally delicious results. The sweet and herbaceous pine nut/currant relish is also a great accompaniment to a simple seared piece of white-fleshed fish, such as bass or branzini.

4–6 SERVINGS

FOR THE PINE NUT/CURRANT RELISH

3 tbsp (24 g) pine nuts, fried in oil
(see page 205)

3 tbsp (28 g) dried currants, plumped in
hot water, drained

1 tbsp (4 g) flat-leaf parsley, finely chopped

3 tbsp (4.8 g) fresh mint, coarsely chopped

1 tbsp (15 ml) sherry vinegar

1 tbsp (15 ml) extra virgin olive oil

Sea salt

FOR THE PRAWNS

12 head-on blue prawns, peeled and
deveined (head and tail intact)

2 tbsp (30 ml) canola oil

2 tbsp (22 g) Harissa (page 186)

Sea salt

Extra virgin olive oil, for garnish

FOR THE PINE NUT/CURRANT RELISH

Toss all the ingredients in a medium bowl and mix thoroughly, season with salt and let the flavors meld for a few hours.

FOR THE PRAWNS

In a large, shallow mixing bowl, gently toss the prawns in the canola oil and harissa. Marinate for 1 hour and up to 6 hours.

Preheat a gas or charcoal grill or grill pan to moderate-high heat.

Bring the prawns to room temperature and season with sea salt. Grill the prawns until firm and charred on the outside, about 2–3 minutes per side.

Arrange the grilled prawns on a platter, top with the pine nut/currant relish and drizzle with olive oil.

> CHEF'S TIP: Be sure to oil the grill well, so the prawns don't stick and tear.

Jerusalem Artichoke Soup with Smoked Salmon and Sumac

Jerusalem artichoke is a misleading name because this vegetable is neither an artichoke nor related to Jerusalem. It is sometimes referred to as a sunchoke, a knobby, tubular root that has a delicate flavor—a little earthy and nutty—making it perfect for this delicately flavored soup. The smoked salmon adds a light smoky note to the soup without overpowering it.

8–10 SERVINGS

½ lb (226g) unsalted butter, diced

1 medium onion, finely chopped

10 garlic cloves, thinly sliced

Sea salt

2 lb (908 g) Jerusalem artichokes, peeled and halved

6 cups (1.4 L) water

3 oz (85 g) high-quality cold-smoked salmon, sliced into bite-size pieces

Ground sumac, for garnish

Chives, finely minced, for garnish

Extra virgin olive oil, for garnish

In a large saucepot, melt half the butter, add the onion and garlic, season with salt and cook over moderate-low heat, stirring often, until the onions are translucent, but not brown, about 5 minutes. Add the Jerusalem artichokes, season with salt and continue to cook over moderately low heat for about 5 minutes, stirring often. Add the water and bring to a boil. Simmer over moderate heat, stirring occasionally, until the Jerusalem artichokes are very tender and the water is just slightly reduced, about 20-30 minutes.

Working in batches, puree the Jerusalem artichokes and the cooking liquid in a blender until smooth; add the rest of the butter in batches, season with salt and reserve warm. Ladle the soup into individual bowls and top with the smoked salmon, a sprinkling of sumac, a few chives and a drizzle of olive oil.

CHEF'S TIP: At Saffron we also garnish the soup with Jerusalem artichoke chips, which are made by soaking very thinly sliced Jerusalem artichokes in salted water for about an hour, patting them dry and frying them at 275-300°F (135-150°C), until crispy. If you want to be fancy, but don't have the time to make your own Jerusalem artichoke chips, you can use high-quality kettle chips.

Sweet Corn Soup with Crab and Spicy Poached Figs

The classic combination of corn and crab is as American as, dare I say, apple pie. Which leads to the question of how is this dish Mediterranean? Although sweet corn is certainly not from the Mediterranean, I grew up eating corn soup. This is a variation on the soup that my mother made. It's been on the menu at Saffron for years. It's so popular that guests alert me when they start seeing the local sweet corn in the farmers' markets. I'm a big fan of pureed soups. The flavors are concentrated, clean and simple. Here, the spicy poached figs, along with the smoked paprika, lend a backbone and lots of textures to this take on the classic American dish.

8 SERVINGS

FOR THE SWEET CORN SOUP

½ lb (226 g) unsalted butter, diced

1 small onion, finely chopped

4 garlic cloves, thinly sliced

Sea salt

8 ears sweet corn, kernels removed, cobs reserved for stock

4 cups (950 ml) Corn Stock (page 178)

FOR THE SPICY POACHED FIGS

8 dried Black Mission figs, tops cut and halved lengthwise

½ cup (120 ml) water

¼ cup (50 g) sugar

½ tsp ground Aleppo chile

½ tsp chile flakes

TO FINISH

½ cup (100 g) Homemade Thick Yogurt (page 189), or Greek yogurt

1 garlic clove, finely grated

1 tsp (5 ml) fresh lemon juice

Sea salt

12 oz (340 g) shelled king crabmeat, about 1¼ lb (567 g) in the shell

¼ cup (43.5 g) Caramelized Paprika Butter (page 176), warmed

2 oz (57 g) corn nuts, lightly crushed

Chives, finely minced, for garnish

FOR THE SWEET CORN SOUP

In a large saucepan, melt half the butter, add the onion and garlic, season with salt and cook over moderate-low heat, stirring, until the onions are translucent, but not brown, about 5–8 minutes. Add the corn kernels, season with salt and continue to cook over moderately low heat for about 5 minutes, stirring often. Add the corn stock and bring to a boil. Simmer over moderate heat, stirring occasionally, until the stock is just slightly reduced, about 20 minutes.

Working in batches, puree the mixture in a blender, on high, until smooth. Add the rest of the butter in batches, season with salt and reserve warm.

FOR THE SPICY POACHED FIGS

In a medium saucepan, combine the figs, water and sugar and bring to a boil. Add the Aleppo chile and chile flakes. Cover and simmer over moderate heat for 15 minutes. Simmer uncovered until the liquid reduces into a glaze and the figs are tender but not mushy, about 15–20 minutes. Let cool completely in the syrup. The poached figs can be refrigerated for up to 1 week. Serve at room temperature.

TO FINISH

In a small bowl, combine the yogurt, garlic and lemon, season with salt and whisk to combine.

Ladle the soup into individual bowls and top with king crab and spicy poached figs. Garnish with a dollop of garlic yogurt, a drizzle of caramelized paprika butter, a sprinkling of crushed corn nuts and a few chives.

CHEF'S TIP: For a variation of this soup, add 1 tablespoon (6.7 g) Ras El Hanout (page 182) to the onion and garlic while they cook. Substitute the Tomato Salad from the Smoky Corn Farina recipe (page 141) for the rest of the garnishes.

Tuna Kubbeh Nayeh

Kubbeh nayeh is essentially tartar, mixed with bulgur wheat, olive oil and dark spices. Traditionally, it's made with either beef or lamb and served with raw vegetables and herbs on the side. Every bite is different, keeping it light and exciting on the palate.

10 SERVINGS

FOR THE KUBBEH NAYEH

¾ cup (114 g) fine bulgur wheat

1½ lb (680 g) high-quality fresh tuna loin, trimmed

1 large shallot, finely minced

½ Preserved Lemon (page 196) rind, finely minced

1½ tsp (4.2 g) Se7en Spice (page 184)

1 tsp (5.2 g) black peppercorns, toasted and ground

1 tsp (2.4 g) ground Aleppo chile

3 tbsp (45 ml) extra virgin olive oil

Sea salt

TO SERVE

3 radishes, sliced into thin rounds

A handful of fresh mint leaves

10 small romaine leaves, washed

3 small Lebanese cucumbers, cut into thick wedges

Crispy Pita Chips (page 179), cut into wedges

Lemon wedges

FOR THE KUBBEH NAYEH

Place the bulgur in a fine-mesh strainer and rinse under running water and rub with fingertips until the water starts to run clear. Drain and place in a medium bowl and let stand for 10–15 minutes. With a fork, fluff and break up the bulgur; it should have softened by this time. If it hasn't, add a few drops of water and let sit for a few more minutes.

Meanwhile, fill a large bowl halfway with ice and place a smaller bowl on top. Place the bulgur in the chilled bowl.

Slice the tuna loin into ¼ inch (6 mm) thin slices. Working in batches, stack the slices and cut into strips and then into small cubes; continue to chop the cubes finely until they begin to stick together and become a little creamy. Place the finely minced tuna into the chilled bowl. Add the shallot, preserved lemon, se7en spice, black pepper and Aleppo chile and mix by hand for 3–4 minutes, adding 2 tablespoons (30 ml) of ice water to make the mixture smooth and creamy. Stir in the olive oil and season liberally with salt.

TO SERVE

Chill a platter in a refrigerator for about 5 minutes. Mound the kubbeh nayeh in the center and garnish the plate with the sliced radishes and mint leaves. Serve with the romaine leaves, cucumber, pita chips and lemons on the side. Use the pita, romaine and cucumber to scoop up the kubbeh nayeh. Top each bite with a mint leaf and a squeeze of lemon.

CHEF'S TIP: You want to be sure to serve the kubbeh nayeh really cold. That's why the mixing bowl is placed on ice to keep it well chilled while it's being prepared.

Beet Salad with Yogurt Cheese & Honey

The combination of earthy beets with the crunchy pistachios, the creamy yogurt cheese and the sweet & sour honey makes for a stunning combination of textures and flavors. The sweet and sour notes of the dish are an oldtime tradition in the Sicilian *agrodolce*. For a different, more refined presentation, roll the yogurt cheese into balls and coat them with the pistachios. You can substitute fresh goat cheese if you are in a pinch.

4 SERVINGS

FOR THE ROASTED BEETS

12 small beets (mixture of golden, Chioggia and red)

3 tbsp (45 ml) olive oil

¼ cup (45 g) kosher salt

1 tbsp (7.6 g) black peppercorns, toasted and ground

2 tbsp (30 ml) good-quality red wine vinegar

FOR THE SWEET & SOUR HONEY

½ cup (120 ml) honey

½ cup (120 ml) good-quality red wine vinegar

Sea salt

TO PLATE

½ cup (120 g) Yogurt Cheese (page 191)

¼ cup (30 g) pistachios, crushed

1 medium head frisee, green tips and thick bottom white parts trimmed

A small handful of small mint leaves, for garnish

Extra virgin olive oil, for garnish

Maldon salt

FOR THE ROASTED BEETS

Preheat the oven to 375°F (190°C). Toss the beets with the olive oil, salt and black pepper. Separate the red beets and place in a baking pan. Place the golden and Chioggia in another pan, making sure that the beets are in a single layer. Cover tightly with foil. Roast for about 1 hour, until tender but not mushy; check by inserting a paring knife into the center of the beets. Remove the pan from the oven; remove the foil from the pan, and let cool at room temperature. Once cooled, starting with the golden beets, gently rub with a paper towel to remove the skin; follow with the Chioggia, then the red. Leave some of the beets whole and cut the rest in half or quarter lengthwise. Toss the beets in the vinegar. Season with salt and reserve.

FOR THE SWEET & SOUR HONEY

In a medium saucepan, place the honey and cook over moderate heat until it turns dark amber in color, about 5 minutes. Add the vinegar, season with a small amount of salt and continue cooking until the mixture has reduced to a syrupy consistency, about 8 minutes. Refrigerate for up to a month. Bring to room temperature before using.

TO PLATE

Arrange a variety of the beets around a platter or individual plates. Drizzle the beets with the sweet & sour honey. Garnish with "crumbles" of yogurt cheese, a sprinkling of pistachios, a few leaves of frisee and mint, a light drizzle of olive oil and a few pinches of crunchy salt.

> **CHEF'S TIP**: Cooking the red beets separately from the golden and Chioggia beets is necessary so that the red beets don't bleed their color all over the other beets.

Wild Arugula Salad with Orange, Medjool Dates and Almonds

I love this combination of flavors. The peppery arugula is a natural pairing with the orange and sweet dates. What really makes the flavors sing is the addition of mint and the spicy harissa. When I was growing up, my mother would gather the wild arugula from friends' houses and make a simple chopped salad with sumac, raw onion and olive oil. I still crave that salad many years later. Wild arugula is much more sharp and peppery than the cultivated varieties of arugula, which can be substituted. Look for younger arugula as a suitable substitute.

4–6 SERVINGS

2 oranges

1 tbsp (11 g) Harissa (recipe 186)

1 tbsp (15 ml) sherry vinegar

1 tbsp (15 ml) orange juice, reserved from cutting segments

2 tbsp (30 ml) extra virgin olive oil

Sea salt

5 oz (142 g) wild arugula

3 tbsp (28.4 g) dried currants

3 tbsp (4.8 g) fresh mint, torn

6 medjool dates, pitted and cut into slivers

3 tbsp (27.3 g) blanched whole almonds, fried in oil (see page 205)

Using a sharp knife, peel the oranges, removing all of the bitter white pith. Working over a bowl, cut in between the membranes to release the sections into the bowl. Squeeze the remainder of the orange over the segments to keep them moist.

In a small mixing bowl, whisk together the harissa, sherry vinegar, reserved orange juice and olive oil; season with salt.

Combine the arugula, currants and mint in a large mixing bowl and drizzle with a small amount of the dressing, season with salt and gently toss to combine. Arrange on a large platter; garnish with the orange segments, dates and whole almonds.

Asparagus Salad with Roasted Garlic and Fresh Cheese

I get excited when spring arrives just to make this recipe. The roasted garlic gives the asparagus a complex richness that pairs beautifully with the oregano and creamy fresh cheese. The roasted garlic vinaigrette makes a perfect sauce for a simple piece of chicken or a grilled steak. As a matter of fact, pair this recipe with the Spice-Crusted Beef Strip Loin (page 113) for a fantastic combination.

6 SERVINGS

FOR THE ROASTED GARLIC VINAIGRETTE

1 head garlic

½ cup (120 ml) canola oil

¼ cup (60 ml) champagne vinegar

½ small shallot, finely minced

¼ cup (60 ml) extra virgin olive oil

Sea salt

Fresh ground black pepper

FOR THE ASPARAGUS SALAD

2 lb (907 g) "jumbo" asparagus, tough bottoms trimmed

1 medium head frisee, green tips and thick bottom white parts trimmed

15 small tomatoes, halved (a mixture of cherry, yellow pear, etc.)

Sea salt

3 oz (85 g) Fresh Cheese (page 179), or store bought

Fresh oregano leaves, for garnish

FOR THE ROASTED GARLIC VINAIGRETTE

Preheat the oven to 325°F (163°C). Cut the top off the head of garlic, just enough to expose the cloves. Place cut-side down in a foil sheet and drizzle with 1 teaspoon (5 ml) of the canola oil and wrap in the foil. Bake in the oven for 20–30 minutes, until the garlic is soft. Remove from the oven and let cool completely. Once cool enough to handle, squeeze out each clove of garlic, place in a small mixing bowl and mash with a fork. Whisk in the champagne vinegar, shallot and slowly drizzle in the olive oil and canola oil while continuing to whisk. Season with sea salt and fresh ground black pepper. Refrigerate extra dressing for future use.

FOR THE ASPARAGUS SALAD

Fill a large bowl with salted ice water. In a large saucepan of salted boiling water, cook the asparagus until they are tender but still crisp, about 2 minutes. Drain immediately and immerse in the salted ice water to cool completely. Drain and pat dry with a paper towel.

In a large bowl, toss the asparagus, frisee and tomatoes, drizzle with a small amount of the roasted garlic vinaigrette and season with salt. On a large platter or individual plates, arrange the asparagus salad in the middle of the plate and garnish with the fresh cheese and oregano.

CHEF'S TIP: You may ask yourself, why salted ice water? Well, I like food that is seasoned well. When submerging perfectly seasoned and blanched vegetables in a pot of water, the salt that's on the outside will be stripped from the vegetables. Adding salt to the ice water makes up for it.

Asparagus with Duck, Gruyère Cheese and Saffron Vinaigrette

Consider making this recipe when asparagus is in season. Out-of-season asparagus is tough, stringy and bland. In this recipe, the contrasting textures of the soft roasted duck and crisp asparagus are really fun, especially when paired with the creamy Gruyère fondue, a great dipping sauce for simply grilled asparagus.

6 SERVINGS

FOR THE SAFFRON VINAIGRETTE

½ tsp saffron threads

¼ cup (60 ml) champagne vinegar

¼ tsp sugar

½ large shallot, finely minced

2 tbsp (30 ml) extra virgin olive oil

½ cup plus 2 tbsp (90 ml) canola oil

Sea salt

FOR THE GRUYÈRE FONDUE

½ cup (120 ml) heavy cream

¼ cup (60 ml) whole milk

1½ cups (162 g) grated aged Gruyère cheese, plus 3 tbsp (7 g) extra, for garnish

1 tbsp (14 g) unsalted butter

Sea salt

FOR THE ROASTED DUCK

3 (8 oz [227 g]) duck legs

½ cup (90 g) kosher salt

1 tsp (2.5 g) black peppercorns, toasted and finely ground

FOR THE ASPARAGUS SALAD

2 lb (907 g) "jumbo" asparagus, tough bottoms trimmed

1 medium head frisee, green tips and thick bottom white parts trimmed

½ bunch (50 g) upland cress leaves

Sea salt

FOR THE SAFFRON VINAIGRETTE

In a small saucepan, toast the saffron over low heat for 20 seconds. Add the champagne vinegar and bring to a simmer, about 1 minute. Add the sugar and let cool completely. Transfer to a small bowl; add the shallot and both oils. Season with salt and whisk to combine.

FOR THE GRUYÈRE FONDUE

In a small saucepan, bring the heavy cream and milk to a boil. Remove the saucepan from the heat and slowly whisk in the Gruyère in small batches, then follow with the butter (using an immersion blender works really well for this). For a smoother texture, place the cream and milk mixture in a blender and slowly add the cheese to combine. Season with salt and reserve warm.

FOR THE ROASTED DUCK

Season the duck with the salt and pepper and refrigerate for 1 hour, or up to 3 hours; this will cure the duck lightly and pull out moisture to help the skin get crispy.

Meanwhile, preheat the oven to 425°F (218°C). Pat the duck dry and set the legs skin side up on a parchment-lined baking sheet. Roast the duck legs in the top third of the oven for 45–60 minutes, until the meat is tender and the skin is crisp. Remove from the oven and cool completely. Remove the skin and snack on it (that's what I do every time I make this recipe). Shred the meat into larger pieces, making sure to discard all the bones; reserve the meat until ready to mix the salad. This can be done up to 2 days in advance.

FOR THE ASPARAGUS SALAD

Fill a large bowl with salted ice water. In a large saucepan of salted boiling water, cook the asparagus until they are tender but still crisp, about 2 minutes. Drain immediately and immerse in the salted ice water to cool completely. Drain and pat dry with a paper towel.

In a large mixing bowl, toss the asparagus, frisee, upland cress and shredded duck, drizzle with a small amount of the saffron vinaigrette and season with salt. On a large platter or individual plates, spoon a generous amount of the Gruyère fondue in the middle of the plate, arrange the asparagus salad in the middle of the plate and garnish with a little more of the saffron vinaigrette and grated Gruyère.

CHEF'S TIP: "Jumbo" asparagus is tougher than standard or thin asparagus, which holds up better in this recipe. If the asparagus is very thick, I like to peel it with a vegetable peeler.

Artichokes with Pecorino and "Barigoule" Vinaigrette

Even though, in the traditional Provençal preparation of barigoule, all the vegetables are cooked together, here the artichokes are cooked separately to keep the flavors clean and more pronounced. The pecorino fondue gives the dish richness and creaminess with a little bit of funk.

6-8 SERVINGS

FOR THE POACHED ARTICHOKES

1 tbsp (15.6 g) citric acid or ¼ cup (60 ml) fresh lemon juice

12 baby artichokes or 3 large artichokes

1 fresh thyme sprig

1 fresh bay leaf

1 cup (240 ml) extra virgin olive oil

1 cup (240 ml) white wine, preferably sauvignon blanc

1 lemon halved

Sea salt

FOR THE PECORINO FONDUTA

½ cup (120 ml) heavy cream

½ cup (38 g) grated Pecorino Romano cheese

A splash of champagne vinegar or lemon juice

FOR THE "BARIGOULE" VINAIGRETTE

1 cup (240 ml) extra virgin olive oil

½ cup (61 g) peeled and thinly sliced carrots

1 small shallot, thinly sliced

2 garlic cloves thinly sliced

1 fresh bay leaf

¼ fresh rosemary sprig

1 fresh thyme sprig

½ cup (120 ml) white wine, preferably sauvignon blanc

Sea salt

Freshly ground black pepper

TO GARNISH

Flat-leaf parsley, finely chopped

Chervil leaves

FOR THE POACHED ARTICHOKES

In a large mixing bowl, whisk 1 cup (240 ml) of water with the citric acid or the lemon juice. Working with 1 artichoke at a time, pull off and discard the dark green outer leaves. Using a sharp paring knife or serrated knife, trim off about ¼ inch (6 mm) of the leaves' tips; peel and trim the ends of the stem, reserving as much of it as possible. Halve the artichoke and scrape out the hairy choke. If using large artichokes, cut off the leaves just above the heart and scoop out the hairy choke. Peel the heart and stem, reserving as much of it as possible. Cut into quarters.

Place the artichoke in the acidulated water. Repeat with the remaining artichokes.

Drain the artichokes and place in a medium saucepot with the thyme, bay leaf, olive oil and white wine. Squeeze the lemon haves and add the juice and lemons. Bring to a simmer over moderately high heat, then reduce the heat to low. Cover and simmer until the artichokes are tender when pierced with a fork, about 15–20 minutes. Let the artichokes cool in the cooking liquid for 30 minutes.

FOR THE PECORINO FONDUTA

In a small saucepan, bring the heavy cream to a boil. Cook over moderate heat until reduced slightly, about 5 minutes. Remove the saucepan from the heat and slowly whisk in the pecorino until melted. Season with the splash of vinegar and reserve warm. Alternatively, place the cream in a blender and slowly add the cheese to combine.

FOR THE "BARIGOULE" VINAIGRETTE

In a medium saucepan, heat 1 tablespoon (15 ml) of the olive oil. Cook the carrots, shallots and garlic for about 2 minutes, until the shallots become translucent, stirring often. Add the bay leaf, rosemary, thyme, white wine and the rest of the olive oil. Continue to cook for 10 minutes over low heat, until the carrots start to soften; season with salt and pepper and reserve.

TO PLATE

Drain the artichokes from the poaching liquid, reserving the liquid for future use. Plate the artichokes; mix the barigoule vinaigrette and spoon liberally on and around the artichokes. Drizzle the warmed pecorino fonduta over the artichokes and garnish with the parsley and a few chervil leaves.

CHEF'S TIP: Reuse the poaching liquid a few more times, adding more white wine and fresh herbs.

Citrus Salad with Medjool Dates and Fennel

The light and refreshing flavors of citrus are paired with sweet dates and crisp, aromatic fennel for a tantalizing flavor combination. The beauty of this salad is in the variety of citrus; you can substitute according to what is available.

8 SERVINGS

1 large fennel bulb

2 blood oranges

1 ruby grapefruit

2 oranges

2 tangerines

1 tbsp (15 ml) sherry vinegar

2 tbsp (30 ml) extra virgin olive oil

Sea salt

Freshly ground black pepper

8 medjool dates, cut into slivers

¼ cup (31 g) pistachios, lightly crushed

Fennel pollen, for garnish

Maldon salt

Cut the fennel bulb in half vertically. Place the fennel half cut-side down on a Japanese mandoline and shave into paper-thin slices. Soak the fennel slices in ice water for 15 minutes, drain and pat dry.

Meanwhile, using a sharp knife, peel the blood orange, grapefruit, oranges and tangerines, removing all of the bitter white pith. Cut the peeled citrus into ¼ inch (6 mm) slices.

Squeeze the peel of the citrus in a small mixing bowl; add the sherry vinegar and olive oil, season with salt and pepper and whisk to combine.

Arrange the slices of citrus and sliced fennel on a large platter or individual plates. Drizzle some of the vinaigrette over the top. Garnish with the medjool dates, pistachios, a light dusting of fennel pollen and a bit of the crunchy salt.

CHEF'S TIP: A trick for cutting dates: make sure that your dates are cold, and dip your knife in hot water before cutting the dates into slivers.

Lentil and Beet Salad with Burrata and Green Charmoula

Lentils are so versatile. One of my favorite ways to serve them is cold in a light, yet full-flavored, autumn salad that can double as a vegetarian entrée. Golden beets have a sweeter, less earthy flavor than the red ones, which works great here, especially when combined with the herbaceous green charmoula.

4 SERVINGS

FOR THE BEETS

12 small golden beets

3 tbsp (45 ml) olive oil

¼ cup (45.2 g) kosher salt

1 tsp (2.5 g) black peppercorns, toasted and ground

FOR THE LENTILS

1 cup (192 g) lentils

½ small onion, halved

1 celery stalk

1 cup (240 ml) vegetable stock

2 cups (480 ml) water

Sea salt

2 tbsp (30 ml) fresh lemon juice

3 tbsp (45 ml) extra virgin olive oil, plus more for drizzling

TO PLATE

½ cup (108 g) Green Charmoula (page 185)

Sea salt

2 (4 oz [114 g]) burrata cheese balls, halved

1 medium head frisee, green tips and thick bottom white parts trimmed

1 cup (20 g) upland cress, leaves trimmed

Maldon salt

FOR THE BEETS

Preheat the oven to 375°F (190°C). Toss the beets with the olive oil, salt and black pepper; place into a baking pan, making sure that the beets are in a single layer. Cover tightly with foil. Roast for about 1 hour, until tender but not mushy; check by inserting a paring knife into the center of the beets. Remove the pan from the oven; remove the foil from the pan and let cool at room temperature. Once cooled, gently rub with a paper towel to remove the skin. Leave some of the beets whole and cut the rest in half or quarter lengthwise.

FOR THE LENTILS

Meanwhile, in a medium saucepan, combine the lentils with the onion, celery, vegetable stock and water. Season with salt and bring to a boil. Simmer over moderate heat until tender, 20 minutes. Drain well and let cool in a large mixing bowl. Remove and discard the onion and celery. Toss with the lemon juice and olive oil and season with salt.

TO PLATE

Spoon the lentils into the center of a platter or individual plates. In a medium-size mixing bowl, toss the beets with 3 tablespoons (41 g) of the green charmoula and season with salt. Arrange the beets and burrata on top of the lentils. Spoon the remaining green charmoula around the plate and garnish with a few leaves of frisee and cress. Finish with a drizzle of olive oil and a sprinkling of Maldon salt.

Blood Orange Salad
with Oil-Cured Black Olives and Mint

Orange, onion and olive are a classic combination from North Africa. Here I pair those flavors with the creamy sheep's milk feta and hot peppers, which work really well against the citrus and pungent olives. Blood oranges have a slightly tart-sweet flavor profile with a subtle berry-like finish. Other, sweeter citrus fruits can be substituted if blood oranges are not available.

4 SERVINGS

4 blood oranges

2 tbsp (30 ml) blood orange juice, reserved from cutting oranges

1 tbsp (15 ml) sherry vinegar

1 tbsp (15 ml) extra virgin olive oil

1 small red onion, peeled, cut into very thin rings ⅛" (3 mm) thick, soaked in ice water for 15 minutes, drained and patted dry

12 oil-cured black olives, pitted and halved

¼ cup (37 g) sheep's milk feta, crumbled

3 tbsp (4.8 g) fresh mint, small leaves

½ jalapeño, very thinly sliced

½ fresno chile, very thinly sliced

Maldon salt

Using a sharp knife, peel the oranges, removing all of the bitter white pith. Cut into horizontal ¼" (6 mm) slices. Squeeze the peel of the orange over the slices to keep them moist. In a small mixing bowl, whisk together the reserved orange juice, sherry vinegar and olive oil.

Arrange the slices of orange on a large platter or individual plates. Drizzle a small amount of the vinaigrette on the oranges. Garnish with the red onion, olives, feta, mint, both chiles and a bit of the crunchy salt.

CHEF'S TIP: I soak the red onion in ice water to make it less pungent and to bring forward the natural sweetness.

Fall Vegetable Fattouch

The word *fattouch* is derived from the Arabic word *fatteh*, which roughly translates to "torn," referring to the bread and vegetables used in this recipe. Traditionally, fattouch is a summer salad. Here, winter vegetables and herbs are used to make it into a fall salad. The lemony sumac-laced vinaigrette is the key to the flavor of this salad.

10 SERVINGS

FOR THE WINTER VEGETABLES

1 cup (100 g) cauliflower, florets

1 cup (140 g) peeled, ½" (13 mm) chunks butternut squash

1 cup (125 g) peeled, ½" (13 mm) chunks carrots

1 cup (133 g) peeled, ½" (13 mm) chunks sweet potatoes

1 cup (125 g) peeled, ½" (13 mm) chunks parsnips

Canola oil

Sea salt

FOR THE SUMAC VINAIGRETTE

2 tbsp (17.5 g) ground sumac

1 tsp (2.8 g) sea salt

1 large shallot, thinly sliced

2 tbsp (30 ml) fresh lemon juice

3 tbsp (45 ml) extra virgin olive oil

FOR THE SALAD

4 pieces Arabic pocket bread (pita), roughly torn into 1½" (4 cm) pieces

4 tbsp (60 ml) olive oil

Sea salt

1 tbsp (8.8 g) ground sumac, plus more for garnish

5 oz (142 g) wild or baby arugula

2 tbsp (4.5 g) fresh oregano, leaves picked

2 tbsp (4.5 g) fresh marjoram, leaves picked

2 tbsp (4 g) fresh thyme, leaves picked

2 tbsp (8 g) flat-leaf parsley, roughly chopped

5 green onions, thinly sliced

FOR THE WINTER VEGETABLES

Preheat the oven to 400°F (205°C). In a large mixing bowl, combine and toss the winter vegetables with the canola oil and season with salt. Spread out the vegetables in one layer on a parchment-lined baking sheet; roast for 20–25 minutes, until they get a light brown color and are semi-soft when pricked with a fork. Keep an eye on the cauliflower, as it might cook faster than the other vegetables and may need to be removed earlier. Remove from the oven and let cool.

FOR THE SUMAC VINAIGRETTE

In a small mixing bowl, combine the sumac, salt and shallots and rub with the tips of your fingers. Add the lemon juice and slowly drizzle in the olive oil while whisking.

FOR THE SALAD

In a medium bowl, toss the pita with the olive oil and season with salt; bake on a parchment-lined baking sheet for 5 minutes, until the pita gets a dark brown color and is crisp. Remove from the heat, return to the mixing bowl, toss with the sumac and let cool completely.

When you are ready to serve, toss the toasted pita with the roasted vegetables, arugula and herbs, drizzle some of the sumac vinaigrette over the mixture and gently toss to mix. Garnish with the green onions and a generous dose of sumac.

CHEF'S TIP: The toasted pita can be stored in an airtight container for up to a week. It also makes an excellent snack on its own or with hummus.

Heirloom Tomato & Melon Salad with Burrata & Skordalia

The inspiration for this salad was the ubiquitous Caprese salad crostini. Skordalia is a Greek garlic dip with many different iterations—potato and garlic, or bread and nuts. Sourdough bread has a nice tang that makes sense as a base for the skordalia. I like to fry the sourdough in oil to intensify the toasty flavors. Sometimes, I use the skordalia as a dipping sauce for fried vegetables and fish. You can also thicken it a little by reducing the amount of liquid in the recipe and serving it as a mezze on its own or with some raw vegetables to dip.

10 SERVINGS

FOR THE SOURDOUGH SKORDALIA

3 tbsp (45 ml) canola oil

¼ cup (60 ml) extra virgin olive oil, plus 3 tbsp (45 ml) for cooking

¼ lb (114 g) day-old sourdough bread, cut into ½" (13 mm) pieces

1½ cups (360 ml) hot water

4 garlic cloves, finely grated

1 tbsp (15 ml) fresh lemon juice

1 tbsp (15 ml) good-quality red wine vinegar

Sea salt

FOR THE LEMON VINAIGRETTE

2 tbsp (30 ml) fresh lemon juice

½ large shallot, finely minced

¼ cup (60 ml) extra virgin olive oil

Sea salt

Freshly ground black pepper

TO PLATE

½ small seedless watermelon

2 small summer melons (cantaloupe, canary, honeydew, crenshaw, preferably two different colors)

5 (4 oz [114 g]) burrata cheese balls, halved

2 lb (907 g) heirloom tomatoes in assorted sizes and colors, cut into different shapes

Chives, cut into 1" (3 cm) pieces, for garnish

Small basil leaves, for garnish

Edible flowers, for garnish, optional

Black pepper

Maldon salt

FOR THE SOURDOUGH SKORDALIA

Heat the canola oil and 3 tablespoons (45 ml) of the olive oil in a medium skillet over moderate heat, add the sourdough and cook for about 2–3 minutes, stirring often, until crisp and golden. Remove the toasted bread with a slotted spoon and place in a medium bowl. Soak the toasted bread in the hot water and cover with plastic film until softened, about 10 minutes.

Transfer the bread to a food processor. Add the garlic, lemon juice and red wine vinegar to the food processor and puree until a paste forms. With the machine on, gradually add the remaining olive oil until incorporated, adding a small amount of water to lightly thin it out if necessary. Season with salt and refrigerate for 1 hour or up to 3 days.

FOR THE LEMON VINAIGRETTE

In a small mixing bowl, whisk all the ingredients, season with salt and pepper and reserve.

TO PLATE

Halve the watermelon and melons, discard the seeds and peel the skin, making sure to keep the melons' round shape. Cut the melon halves into different shapes and sizes, such as half moons, full moons and cubes.

Spoon a generous amount of the skordalia on individual plates or a large platter and spread in a circle with the back of the spoon. Place the burrata in the center of the plate and arrange the tomatoes and melons around. Spoon a small amount of the lemon vinaigrette on the tomatoes, melons and burrata, and garnish with the chives, a few leaves of basil and the edible flowers, if using. Season the burrata with a few coarse grinds of black pepper and finish with a sprinkling of crunchy salt on the tomatoes and burrata.

Poached Pear Salad with Celery Root, Manchego and Bastirma

Bastirma is a spiced and air-cured beef ham that is very popular in the Levant and Turkey. It lends a salty, slightly funky profile to the dish. Celery root or celeriac is an underappreciated vegetable that has a very distinct and intense flavor. It is almost a cross between celery and parsley, which tends to work well with strong flavors such as the bastirma and the sweet poached pears.

6 SERVINGS

FOR THE SHERRY VINAIGRETTE

2 tbsp (30 ml) aged sherry vinegar

¼ cup (60 ml) extra virgin olive oil

Sea salt

FOR THE SHERRY-POACHED PEAR

2 cups (480 ml) water

1½ cups (360 ml) oloroso sherry

1 cup (200 g) sugar

1 tsp (2.6 g) black peppercorns

3 star anise pods

1 stick of cinnamon

3 cardamom pods, lightly crushed

3 Bosc pears

FOR THE SALAD

2 tbsp (30 ml) canola oil

1 medium celery root, peeled, washed and cut into ½" (13 mm) dice

4 cups (75 g) baby kale

Sea salt

1 cup (116 g) crumbled Manchego cheese

3 tbsp (9 g) finely chopped chives

1 cup (20 g) mint leaves, torn

1 tbsp (15 ml) fresh lemon juice

1 tbsp (15 ml) extra virgin olive oil

1 oz (28 g) bastirma, sliced paper thin

¼ cup (34 g) hazelnuts, roasted, hulled and crushed lightly (see page 205)

FOR THE SHERRY VINAIGRETTE

In a small bowl, combine the sherry vinegar and olive oil, season with salt and whisk to combine. This is not an emulsified vinaigrette, so you will have to whisk it just prior to using it.

FOR THE SHERRY-POACHED PEARS

Combine the water, sherry, sugar, black peppercorns, star anise, cinnamon and cardamom in a medium saucepot and bring to a simmer over moderate-high heat.

Meanwhile, peel and cut the pears in half, remove the cores of the pears with a melon baller and cut each half into quarters. Place the pear pieces in the simmering liquid and cover with a parchment paper circle. Reduce the heat to low and continue to cook gently until the pears are cooked through and are soft when pierced with the tip of a knife, about 15–20 minutes. Remove from the heat and leave to cool, uncovered. Refrigerate in the poaching liquid for up to 1 week in an airtight container. The poaching liquid can be reserved and reused for future use.

FOR THE SALAD

In a large, deep skillet, heat the canola oil. Add the celery root and season lightly with salt. Cook over moderate heat, stirring occasionally, until lightly browned in spots and tender, about 10–13 minutes. Remove from the heat and drain the celery root on an absorbent towel until cool to the touch.

In a large bowl, toss the kale with a small amount of the sherry vinaigrette and season with salt. Arrange the kale in the center of a large platter or individual plates.

Combine the poached pears, celery root, Manchego cheese, chives and mint with the lemon juice and olive oil, season with salt and toss gently in a mixing bowl. Arrange on top the kale and garnish with the bastirma, hazelnuts and a drizzle of the sherry vinaigrette around the plate.

Poached Quince Salad with Radicchio and Roasted Duck

Most varieties of quince are too hard and astringent to eat raw. Here the quince is slow cooked in a spiced honey syrup until the flesh turns to a rosy pink. The honey, musk and rose perfume of the quince adds an ethereal element to this salad, especially when paired with the honey-laced vinaigrette. The poached quince also makes a great dessert. Reduce the poaching liquid to a glaze and toss the poached quince in it to coat and serve with a scoop of ice cream.

6 SERVINGS

FOR THE HONEY VINAIGRETTE

2 tbsp (42 g) honey, warmed

2 tbsp (30 ml) champagne vinegar

½ small shallot, finely minced

¼ cup (60 ml) extra virgin olive oil

Sea salt

FOR THE POACHED QUINCE

3 cups (720 ml) water

1 cup (340 g) honey

½ lemon, juiced

1 stick of cinnamon

3 cardamom pods, lightly crushed

3 large quinces

FOR THE ROASTED DUCK

3 (8 oz [227 g]) duck legs

¼ cup (45 g) kosher salt

1 tbsp (8.4 g) Garam Masala (page 181)

FOR THE SALAD

1 large radicchio, torn into bite-size pieces

A large handful of wild or baby arugula

Sea salt

FOR THE HONEY VINAIGRETTE

In a small mixing bowl, combine the honey and champagne vinegar and whisk until the honey is dissolved. Add the shallots and olive oil, season with salt and whisk to combine.

FOR THE POACHED QUINCE

Combine the water, honey, lemon half and juice, cinnamon and cardamom in a medium saucepot and bring to a simmer over moderate-high heat.

Meanwhile, peel and cut the quince in half. Remove the cores of the quince with a melon baller, making sure to remove all fibrous parts. Place the peeled quince halves in the simmering liquid and cover with a parchment paper circle. Reduce the heat to low and continue to cook gently until the quince are cooked through and are soft when pierced with the tip of a knife, about 60–70 minutes. (If the quince is not fully ripe, it will take longer.) Remove from the heat and leave to cool, uncovered. Refrigerate in the poaching liquid for up to 1 week in an airtight container. The poaching liquid can be reused.

FOR THE ROASTED DUCK

Season the duck with the salt and garam masala and refrigerate for 1 hour and up to 3 hours. This will cure the duck lightly and pull out moisture to help the skin get crispy.

Meanwhile, preheat the oven to 425°F (218°C). Brush off the extra salt, pat the duck dry and set the legs skin side up on a parchment-lined baking tray. Roast the duck legs in the top third of the oven for 45–60 minutes, until the meat is tender and the skin is crisp. Remove from the oven and cool completely. Remove the skin and chop it up into small pieces. Shred the meat into larger pieces, making sure to discard all the bones. Reserve the skin and meat until ready to mix the salad.

FOR THE SALAD

In a large bowl, toss the radicchio, arugula and shredded duck, drizzle with a small amount of the honey vinaigrette and season with salt. Quarter the quince halves. On a large platter or individual plates, arrange the salad in the middle of the plate and garnish with the quince.

CHEF'S TIP: If you can't find quince, you can substitute apples or pears. Add a few drops of rose water and one dried hibiscus flower to the poaching liquid and reduce the cooking time to 10–13 minutes as apples and pears cook much quicker.

Lobster & Winter Vegetable "Panzanella"

Inspired by the Tuscan bread salad, this recipe is guaranteed to be a part of your repertoire for years to come. The sweetness of the lobster meat really works well against the roasted vegetables and the smoky paprika soaked croutons.

4 SERVINGS

FOR THE POACHED LOBSTER

3 tbsp (45 ml) champagne vinegar

¼ cup (45.2 g) kosher salt

2 (1½ lb [680 g]) live lobsters

FOR THE WINTER VEGETABLES

½ cup (50 g) cauliflower florets

½ cup (70 g) peeled, 1" (3 cm) diced butternut squash

½ cup (78 g) peeled, 1" (3 cm) diced celery root

½ cup (67 g) peeled, 1" (3 cm) diced sweet potatoes

½ cup (63 g) peeled, 1" (3 cm) diced parsnips

Olive oil

Sea salt

FOR THE HERB VINAIGRETTE

1 large shallot, finely chopped

2 garlic cloves, finely chopped

1 tbsp (15 ml) fresh lemon juice

1 tbsp (15 ml) good-quality red wine vinegar

1 tbsp (3 g) chives, finely chopped

1 tbsp (2 g) fresh thyme leaves, finely chopped

3 tbsp (45 ml) extra virgin olive oil

Sea salt

FOR THE CROUTONS

4 cups (450 g) roughly torn into 1" (3 cm) pieces, ciabatta or other rustic white bread

¼ cup (60 ml) extra virgin olive oil

1 tsp (2.7 g) Spanish sweet smoked paprika

Sea salt

FOR THE SALAD

2 ½ cups (70 g) wild or baby arugula

2 tbsp (4 g) fresh thyme, leaves picked, plus more for garnish

Maldon salt

Freshly ground black pepper

FOR THE POACHED LOBSTER

Fill a small stockpot with water, add the vinegar and salt and bring to a boil over moderate-high heat. Lay the lobsters on a cutting board. Place one hand on the tail and hold it flat against the board. With the other hand, place the tip of a large sharp knife about 1 inch (3 cm) behind the eyes, where the body meets the tail, with the blade facing head. In one quick motion, plunge the tip of the knife straight down through the head and bring the blade down to the board to kill the lobster instantly. Reduce the heat under the boiling water to maintain a simmer, drop the lobsters in the water, cover and cook gently until the shell is bright red, 9–12 minutes.

While the lobsters cook, fill a large bowl with equal amounts of ice and water. Carefully remove the lobsters from the pot and plunge into the ice water and completely cool; drain. Twist the tails off of the lobster bodies; crack the claws and knuckles and remove the meat. Using scissors, cut along the underside of the tail shells and remove the meat. Remove and discard the dark intestinal veins; cut the tails into 2 inch (5 cm) pieces and reserve in a bowl with the claws and knuckles.

FOR THE WINTER VEGETABLES

Preheat the oven to 400°F (205°C). In a large bowl, combine and toss the winter vegetables with the olive oil and season with salt. Spread out the vegetables in one layer on a parchment-lined baking sheet, and roast for 20–25 minutes, until they get a light brown color and are semi-soft when pricked with a fork. Keep an eye on the cauliflower as it might cook faster than the other vegetables and may need to be removed earlier. Remove from the oven and let cool.

FOR THE HERB VINAIGRETTE

In a small bowl, combine all the ingredients, season with salt and reserve.

FOR THE CROUTONS

In a medium bowl, toss the bread with the olive oil and paprika, season with salt and bake on a parchment-lined baking sheet for 5–7 minutes, or until the bread gets a golden color and is crisp on the outside, but soft within. Remove from the heat and cool completely. Store in an airtight container for up to 4 days.

FOR THE SALAD

Toss 2 tablespoons (30 ml) of the vinaigrette over the lobster and gently mix. When you are ready to serve, gently toss and combine the roasted vegetables, croutons, arugula and thyme with the lobster and lightly coat with the remaining vinaigrette. Garnish with the crunchy salt, black pepper and reserved thyme leaves.

Romaine Salad with Feta & Peppercorn Dressing

I love romaine and so should you. It's crisp and sturdy and has the ability to stand up to the creamy vinaigrette, which is not a common thing in the Mediterranean. The feta and peppercorn vinaigrette is very simple to make and works really well with any type of lettuce or greens. The Szechuan pepper, although not traditional in Mediterranean cuisine, has become a staple in my spice cabinet. It produces a tingling, numbing sensation on the tongue with a slightly lemony undertone.

6 SERVINGS

FOR THE FETA & PEPPERCORN
VINAIGRETTE

1 small shallot, minced

¼ cup (60 ml) fresh lemon juice

7 oz (198 g) sheep's milk feta

½ tsp pink peppercorns

½ tsp Szechuan pepper

¼ tsp black peppercorns, cracked

½ cup (120 ml) extra virgin olive oil

¼ cup (60 ml) canola oil

Sea salt

FOR THE SALAD

3 (13 oz [370 g]) romaine hearts, halved
lengthwise

9 Peppadew peppers, halved

3 cups (492 g) Cooked Chickpeas (page
204), preferably multicolored, cold

1 medium watermelon radish, peeled and
thinly sliced

Crispy Pita Chips (page 179), for garnish

Flat-leaf parsley leaves, for garnish

FOR THE FETA & PEPPERCORN VINAIGRETTE

Place all the ingredients except the olive oil and canola oil in a blender and puree until smooth; slowly drizzle in the oils until well blended. Taste and adjust the seasoning with more lemon and salt if necessary. The vinaigrette should be slightly salty and have an assertive lemon flavor.

FOR THE SALAD

Arrange the romaine hearts on individual plates or a large platter; spoon a generous amount of the vinaigrette on top. Garnish with the Peppadew peppers, cooked chickpeas, watermelon radishes, a handful of pita chips and a few leaves of parsley.

CHEF'S TIP: Peppadew is a brand name for a pickled sweet and mild chile pepper that is native to South Africa. The flavor is a cross between a tomato and a sweet pepper and the size is that of a cherry tomato. At Saffron, we puree some of the peppers in a blender with a small amount of water and use the puree to garnish the plate.

Summer Melon Salad with Basil, Almonds and Goat's Milk Yogurt

I love melons. The flavor and soft texture are perfect for a variety of preparations. In this dish, I combine the melons with goat's milk yogurt, which adds a beautiful creamy acidic note to the sweet summer melons, while the almond gives the salad a nutty flavor and crunchy texture.

8 SERVINGS

FOR THE SUMMER MELON

2 small summer melons (cantaloupe, canary, honeydew, crenshaw, preferably two different colors)

½ small seedless watermelon

FOR THE ARUGULA SALAD

2 cups (70 g) wild or baby arugula

1 medium head frisee, green tips and thick, white bottom parts trimmed

½ cup (12 g) small basil leaves

1 tbsp (15 ml) fresh lemon juice

3 tbsp (45 ml) extra virgin olive oil

Sea salt

Freshly ground black pepper

TO FINISH

1 cup (200 g) goat's milk yogurt

¼ cup (68 g) soft goat cheese, at room temperature

3 tbsp (27 g) blanched whole almonds, fried, crushed (see page 205)

Urfa pepper, for garnish

Maldon salt

FOR THE SUMMER MELON

Halve the melons, discard the seeds and peel the skin, making sure to keep the melons' round shape. Cut the melon halves into different shapes and sizes, such as half moons, full moons and cubes. Peel the watermelon and cut into different shapes and sizes.

FOR THE ARUGULA SALAD

Just prior to serving, combine the arugula, frisee and basil in a medium bowl, toss together with the lemon juice and olive oil and season with salt and pepper to taste.

TO FINISH

In a medium bowl, combine the yogurt and the goat cheese and whisk until there are no lumps. Spoon the yogurt/cheese mixture onto a large platter and spread with the back of the spoon. Mound the arugula salad in the middle and arrange the melons around the salad in an artful way. Top with the crushed almonds and Urfa pepper and season the melons with the Maldon salt. Serve right away.

Large Plates

In this chapter, I have taken creative liberties with traditional dishes like beef tangia and updated classics such as chicken kebobs. These recipes range from the simple and quick Spice Crusted Beef Strip Loin (page 113) to the more complex and time-consuming—but totally worth it—Chicken Bastela (91).

Large plates and "one-pot meals" are an ancient culinary tradition of the Mediterranean. As the center of the meal, some are served as a stand-alone dish, and others alongside salads, mezze and side dishes. The dishes in this chapter showcase meat, poultry and seafood.

Beef Short Rib & Root Vegetable Tangia

Traditionally, this unique Marrakesh "bachelor's stew" of slow-cooked meat is prepared in a clay pot called a *tangia*. Typically, men would prepare the tangia and bring it to an oven adjacent to a *hammam* (men's public bathhouse), where it would slow cook in the ashes from the fire used to heat the bathhouse. Don't panic if you don't have a tangia or a bathhouse. You can recreate the dish using another ovenproof clay pot, a Dutch oven or a deep cast-iron casserole. Just like all slow-cooked dishes, the beef and vegetables get a concentrated rich, deep flavor from the aromatic spices stewing within the sauce. Think pot roast with robust and fragrant aromas and tastes.

6 SERVINGS

FOR THE BEEF SHORT RIBS

6 English cut beef short ribs, excess fat trimmed (about 4 lb [1.8 kg] total)

Sea salt

Canola oil

2 small yellow onions, coarsely chopped

½ cup (68 g) garlic cloves, sliced

¼ cup (28 g) grated fresh ginger

2 tbsp (13.3 g) Ras El Hanout (page 182)

1 tbsp (8 g) Spanish smoked sweet paprika

2 tsp (4 g) ground ginger

1 tbsp (7.5 g) black peppercorns, toasted and ground

1 cinnamon stick

3 star anise pieces

6–8 cups (1.4–1.9 L) chicken stock or water

12 cilantro sprigs

2 fresh bay leaves

1 tbsp (18 g) Preserved Lemon "Plazma" (page 199), or 1 tbsp (15 ml) fresh lemon juice mixed with a pinch of Spice Salt (page 184)

FOR THE VEGETABLES

6 small turnips, peeled and halved

12 small fingerling potatoes, preferably multicolored

2 small parsnips, peeled and cut into 1" (3 cm) pieces

2 small carrots, peeled and cut into 1" (3 cm) pieces

Canola oil

Sea salt

TO FINISH

¼ cup (17 g) cilantro, roughly chopped

½ Preserved Lemon rind (page 196) thinly sliced

Maldon salt

FOR THE BEEF SHORT RIBS

Preheat the oven to 325°F (163°C). Season the short ribs generously with salt. Heat a thin film of the canola oil in a large enameled cast-iron casserole. Working in batches, brown the short ribs thoroughly over moderately high heat, turning often, about 4 minutes per side. Transfer the short ribs to a baking sheet.

Add the onion, garlic and grated ginger to the casserole, season with salt and cook over moderate heat, stirring occasionally, for about 5 minutes, until the onions start to become translucent. Add the ras el hanout, paprika, ginger powder, black pepper, cinnamon stick and star anise. Cook for 1 minute, stirring continuously to bring out the flavor of the spices. Deglaze with a small amount of the stock or water and bring to a boil, about 1–2 minutes, using a wooden spatula to scrape up the browned bits from the bottom of the casserole. Tie the cilantro and bay leaves together with kitchen twine to form an herb bundle.

Return the short ribs, bone side down, and any drippings from the baking sheet to the casserole. Add the rest of the stock or water and preserved lemon "plazma." Bring to a boil, then cover and cook in the preheated oven for 2–3 hours, or until the short ribs are very tender. Remove the casserole from the oven.

FOR THE VEGETABLES

Meanwhile, in a large bowl, combine the vegetables and toss with a small amount of oil, season with salt, spread on a parchment-lined baking sheet and roast until the vegetables are semi-tender, about 30 minutes.

TO FINISH

Carefully transfer the short ribs to a baking sheet and cover with foil. Let the cooking liquid stand for 5 minutes, and then skim off the fat that has risen to the top. Remove and discard the cinnamon stick, star anise and herb bundle. Combine the roasted vegetables with the sauce and simmer over moderate to low heat until reduced by half, stirring frequently, about 20 minutes. Return the short ribs to the sauce, bring to a simmer and adjust the seasoning with salt.

Set the beef short ribs on a platter or individual plates, arrange the vegetables around the short ribs and drizzle with the sauce. Sprinkle with the cilantro, preserved lemon slices and Maldon salt.

Chicken Bastela

At first glance this recipe may seem odd (powdered sugar on a chicken dish??), but the balance of the savory flavors with sweet spices and sugar really hits the mark.

4–6 SERVINGS

FOR THE STEWED CHICKEN

6 skin-on, bone-in chicken thighs (about 2½ lb [1.2 kg] total)

2 tsp (4.5 g) Ras El Hanout (page 182)

1 tsp (0.9 g) saffron threads

4 garlic cloves, finely grated

¼ small onion, finely grated

2 tbsp (16.8 g) sea salt

2 cinnamon sticks

1½ cups (360 ml) chicken stock or water

FOR THE FILLING

2 cups (348 g) Clarified Butter or Ghee (page 203)

4 small onions, thinly sliced

¼ cup (34 g) garlic cloves, finely chopped

1½ tsp (3.4 g) Ras El Hanout (page 182)

½ tsp (1.3 g) ground cinnamon

¼ tsp (0.7 g) grated nutmeg

Sea salt

¼ cup (60 ml) fresh lemon juice

8 egg yolks, beaten

¼ cup (17 g) cilantro, chopped

¼ cup (17 g) flat-leaf parsley, chopped

TO FINISH

8 oz (227 g) (about 10 sheets) phyllo dough, thawed

2 cups (276 g) whole, skin-on almonds, fried in oil and crushed (see page 205)

1 tsp (3 g) confectioner's sugar

1 tsp (2.6 g) ground cinnamon

½ cup (12 g) cilantro, leaves only

¼ cup (6 g) flat-leaf parsley, leaves only

½ cup (12 g) mint, leaves only

2 green onions, thinly sliced on the diagonal

¼ Preserved Lemon rind (page 196), thinly sliced

Sea salt

Extra virgin olive oil

FOR THE STEWED CHICKEN

Preheat the oven to 350°F (177°C). In a large, ovenproof casserole, mix the chicken with the ras el hanout, saffron, garlic, onion and salt. Add the cinnamon sticks and stock or water and bring to a simmer over moderate heat. Cover with foil and place in the oven and cook for 1–1½ hours, until the chicken cooks through and the bone pulls easily from the meat. Remove the chicken and set aside, then strain the liquid and reserve. Discard the cinnamon sticks. Once the chicken is cool enough to handle, shred the chicken meat with your hands into large chunks. Remove and discard the bones and skin.

FOR THE FILLING

Heat ½ cup (90 g) of the clarified butter in a large saucepan. Add the sliced onions and cook over moderate heat for 8–10 minutes, stirring occasionally. Add the garlic and spices, season with salt and cook for another 5 minutes, stirring often. Add 2 cups (480 ml) of the reserved cooking liquid, bring to simmer and reduce, uncovered, to about 1¼ cups (300 ml). Increase the heat to moderately high and add the lemon juice. Slowly stir in the egg yolks, while stirring continuously, until the eggs cook and thicken the sauce, about 2 minutes. Add the shredded chicken, cilantro and parsley and coat with the egg sauce. Adjust the seasoning with salt and let cool.

TO ASSEMBLE

Increase the oven temperature to 400°F (205°C). Warm the remaining clarified butter in a small saucepan. Unroll the phyllo dough, keeping it under a damp towel to prevent it from drying out. Brush some of the butter over the bottom and sides of a 9 inch (23 cm) pie pan. Brush 1 piece of phyllo with butter and fold in half and place the fold in the center of the pie pan to give you a 4" (10 cm) overhang. Repeat with 3–4 more pieces of phyllo, overlapping each by about half to completely cover the bottom of the pan, while brushing each layer with butter.

Spread the cooled chicken mixture on the bottom of the pan in an even layer and top with the almonds. Fold over the overlapping sheets of phyllo toward the center. Continue with all the sheets until the bastela is completely encased in phyllo. Place 2 sheets of phyllo as a top layer, brush with butter and fold the edges onto the bastela.

TO FINISH

Bake for 30–40 minutes, or until the phyllo bastela is golden brown and crisp. Remove from the oven and cool for 10 minutes. Invert the bastela onto a sheet pan to catch any excess butter. Transfer to a serving platter and blot the surface with paper towels. Dust with the sugar, then run crisscrossing lines of cinnamon over the top.

Right before serving the bastela, toss all the rest of the herbs and preserved lemon in a small mixing bowl; season with salt and a drizzle of olive oil. Garnish the side of the bastela with the herb salad and serve immediately.

Braised Chicken & Prawns with Smoked Paprika and Sherry

This is a sort of surf-and-turf inspired by Spanish flavors. The chicken absorbs the rich flavors of the sherry and paprika while slowly cooking in the vinegar-laced sauce. Spanish smoked paprika or pimentón has a warm, smoky and rounded flavor that comes from smoke-drying the red peppers over oak fires. Pimentón comes in three different types or heat levels: dulce or sweet, which is mild and light orange; agridulce or medium hot, which is darker and spicier; and picante or hot, which is typically made from a combination of different types of peppers and is darker red and spicy. For this recipe we combine the sweet and hot paprika. You can skip the hot paprika and add a pinch of cayenne, if you want it milder.

6 SERVINGS

Canola oil

6 skin-on, bone-in chicken thighs (about 3 lbs [1.36 kg] total)

Sea salt

Freshly ground black pepper

½ cup (68 g) garlic cloves, thinly sliced

1 tbsp (14 g) unsalted butter

2 tbsp (16 g) all-purpose flour

2 tbsp (16 g) Spanish sweet smoked paprika, plus more for garnish

2 tsp (5.4 g) Spanish hot smoked paprika

1 cinnamon stick

4 fresh bay leaves

1½ cups (360 ml) amontillado sherry

⅓ cup (80 ml) sherry vinegar

3 cups (720 ml) chicken stock or water

1 cup (250 g) San Marzano tomatoes, crushed

6 large head-on prawns

¼ cup (17 g) flat-leaf parsley, roughly chopped

Preheat the oven to 350°F (177°C).

In a large, enameled cast-iron skillet or medium casserole, heat 2 tablespoons (30 ml) of canola oil until shimmering. Season the chicken thighs generously with salt and black pepper. Place the chicken thighs, skin-side down, in the skillet and cook over moderate heat until golden brown, about 3 minutes per side. Transfer the chicken thighs to a plate. Add 1 tablespoon (15 ml) of oil and the garlic to the skillet and cook over moderate heat, stirring continuously for about 5 minutes, until the garlic is toasted and starts to brown lightly. Add the butter to the pan and melt over moderate heat, then add the flour and stir continuously for 30 seconds. Add both paprikas, the cinnamon stick and the bay leaves, and cook for 30 seconds, stirring continuously to bring out the flavor of the spices. Stir in the amontillado sherry and bring to a boil, about 1 minute, using a wooden spatula to scrape up the browned bits from the bottom of the skillet. Add the sherry vinegar, chicken stock and crushed tomatoes, season with salt and bring to a boil.

Nestle the chicken thighs, skin-side up, and any drippings in the skillet. Transfer the skillet to the oven and braise, uncovered, for about 1 hour, until the chicken thighs are very tender.

Meanwhile, peel the prawns, leaving the head and tail intact. Run a sharp paring knife down the back of each prawn, just deep enough to be able to remove and discard the vein. Season the prawns with salt, nestle the prawns in the sauce around the chicken thighs and continue to cook for about 5–8 minutes, until they are cooked through. Remove from the oven and let rest for a few minutes. Discard the cinnamon stick and bay leaves and garnish with the parsley and a light dusting of paprika.

Braised Veal Breast with Preserved Lemon

Veal is not a very popular meat in the United States, but it should be, as it's a perfect blank canvas for any flavor combination. The preserved lemon "plazma" adds a slightly bitter and very distinct briny-citrusy note to the braising liquid, while the gremolata balances out the richness of the veal with some herbaceousness and a hint of spice.

6 SERVINGS

FOR THE VEAL BREAST

1 (3–4 lb [1.3–1.8 kg]) veal breast, boneless and trimmed

Sea salt

Canola oil

6 cups (690 g) coarsely chopped yellow onion

½ cup (74 g) garlic cloves, coarsely chopped

¼ cup (28 g) coarsely chopped fresh ginger

4 tbsp (16 g) coriander seeds, toasted and ground

3 tbsp (18 g) cumin seeds, toasted and ground

1 tbsp (7.5 g) black peppercorns, toasted and ground

2 cups (480 ml) dry white wine

2 bay leaves

12 flat-leaf parsley sprigs

8 thyme sprigs

8 cups (1.9 L) rich chicken stock, veal stock or water

¼ cup (72 g) Preserved Lemon "Plazma" (page 199)

3 tbsp (45 ml) Preserved Lemon juice (page 196)

FOR THE PRESERVED LEMON GREMOLATA

½ finely diced Preserved Lemon rind (page 196)

1 garlic clove, finely grated

1 cup (67 g) flat-leaf parsley, finely chopped

2 tsp (5 g) black peppercorns, toasted and coarsely ground

2 tbsp (8 g) coriander seeds, toasted and coarsely ground

FOR THE TOASTED BREADCRUMBS

¼ cup (60 ml) olive oil

1 cup (64 g) panko bread crumbs

Sea salt

FOR THE VEAL BREAST

Preheat the oven to 325°F (163°C). Season the veal breast generously with salt. Heat a thin film of the canola oil in a large enameled cast-iron casserole, over moderately high heat. Add the veal breast, fat side down, and sear for about 5 minutes, pressing it down from time to time. Once the bottom has browned, turn the meat over and brown for another 5 minutes. Transfer the veal to a baking sheet. Add the onion, garlic and ginger to the casserole, season with salt and cook over moderate heat, stirring occasionally, for about 5 minutes, until the onions start to become translucent. Add the coriander, cumin and black pepper; cook for 30 seconds, stirring continuously, to bring out the flavor of the spices. Deglaze with the wine and bring to a boil, about 3 minutes, using a wooden spatula to scrape up the browned bits from the bottom of the casserole.

Tie the bay leaves, parsley and thyme sprigs together with kitchen twine to form an herb bundle. Return the veal and any drippings from the baking sheet to the casserole. Add the stock or water, herb bundle and preserved lemon "plazma". Bring to a boil, then cover and cook in the preheated oven for 2½–3½ hours, or until the veal is very tender, cooking the meat uncovered for the last 30 minutes. Remove the casserole from the oven and let the meat rest in the pot for 30 minutes.

Carefully transfer the veal to a parchment-lined baking sheet and cover with another layer of parchment. Top with a second baking sheet and put a weight on top. Refrigerate until completely cooled, about 4 hours or up to 24 hours. Meanwhile, let the cooking liquid stand for 5 minutes and then skim off the fat that has risen to the top. Remove and discard the herb bundle. Simmer the sauce over moderate to low heat until reduced by half, stirring frequently, about 20 minutes. Season the sauce with the preserved lemon juice and salt if necessary. Place the cooled veal on a cutting board and cut into 6 equally sized pieces. Return the veal pieces to the sauce and bring to a simmer, while spooning some of the sauce on top, until the meat is richly glazed.

FOR THE PRESERVED LEMON GREMOLATA

In a small mixing bowl, combine all ingredients and reserve.

FOR THE TOASTED BREADCRUMBS

Heat the olive oil in a medium frying pan over moderate heat. Add the breadcrumbs and cook for about 4 minutes, until they are deep brown. Season with a small amount of salt and drain on paper towels.

TO PLATE

Set the veal breast on a platter or individual plates. Spoon the sauce over the meat and sprinkle with the preserved lemon gremolata and toasted breadcrumbs.

Charcoal Grilled Chicken Skewers in Ancient Arab Spices

Using yogurt and grated onion to marinating poultry is a technique that I learned from my mother. By marinating for a long period of time, the acid in the yogurt helps break down the connective tissue of the meat and allows moisture to be absorbed. As the yogurt cooks, it caramelizes and seals the meat and gives it a great charred exterior and flavor. This fragrant marinade can be used on any meat or poultry.

4 SERVINGS

FOR THE MARINATED CHICKEN

4 boneless, skinless chicken thigh or breast meat (1½ lbs [680 g] total)

¼ cup (50 g) Homemade Thick Yogurt (page 189), or Greek yogurt

¼ cup (60 ml) canola oil, plus extra for grilling

2 garlic cloves, finely grated

¼ small yellow onion, finely grated

3 tbsp (16 g) Ancient Arab Spice Blend (page 174)

1½ tbsp (23 ml) Saffron Water (page 199)

2 tsp (10 ml) sherry vinegar

1 tbsp (15 ml) fresh lemon juice

Sea salt

FOR THE CILANTRO YOGURT SAUCE

½ cup (100 g) Homemade Thick Yogurt (page 189), or Greek yogurt

1 tbsp (4 g) cilantro, roughly chopped

1 tbsp (15 ml) fresh lemon juice

A pinch of cayenne

Sea salt

FOR THE MARINATED CHICKEN

Trim the chicken of excess fat. If using breasts, remove the tenders and reserve for another use. Cut the meat into 1½ inch (4 cm) pieces. Whisk the rest of the ingredients in a large mixing bowl. Toss the chicken in the marinade and refrigerate for a minimum of 3 hours and up to overnight.

FOR THE CILANTRO YOGURT SAUCE

Whisk all the ingredients in a small mixing bowl, then season with salt. Can be made up to 6 hours in advance.

FOR THE SKEWERS

Use 4 thin metal skewers or if not available, soak long wooden skewers in cold water for 30 minutes. Preheat the charcoal grill to medium-high heat or you can use a gas grill, but the flavor won't be as good.

Squeeze the chicken to drain the extra marinade. Skewer the chicken and season with sea salt. Generously oil the grill with the reserved oil, as the marinade makes it easy for the chicken to stick to the grill. Grill the skewers for 3–5 minutes without moving them, until well browned on the outside. Turn the skewers over and cook for about 2 minutes to finish cooking the chicken. Let rest for 3 minutes. Serve with the cilantro yogurt sauce.

CHEF'S TIP: Like most chefs, I feel that chicken thighs have more flavor than the breasts. If you use breast meat, be careful not to overcook, as it tends to dry out quickly, but I'm sure you already knew that.

Duck Kefta Tagine with Sweet & Spicy Tomato Sauce

Kefta is typically made with lamb or beef. In this variation on the classic North African dish, it's made with ground duck meat and the heady spice flavors of ras el hanout and smoked paprika. The kefta then gets roasted and finishes cooking in a tagine, in a tomato sauce that is sweet, sour and a little spicy. The egg yolk is not supposed to cook through; it should get stirred into the dish to add creaminess and richness.

6–8 SERVINGS

FOR THE DUCK KEFTA

½ small onion, roughly chopped

1 tbsp (6 g) finely grated fresh ginger

6 garlic cloves, roughly chopped

¼ cup (15 g) cilantro, roughly chopped

½ tbsp (8 ml) red wine vinegar

1 tbsp (8 g) Spanish smoked hot paprika

1½ tbsp (10 g) Ras El Hanout (page 182)

2 cups (128 g) panko breadcrumbs

2 lb (907 g) ground duck

2 eggs

Sea salt

FOR THE SWEET & SPICY TOMATO SAUCE

1 tbsp (15 ml) canola oil

½ small onion, finely diced

4 garlic cloves, thinly sliced

Sea salt

3 tbsp (45 ml) red wine vinegar

3 tbsp (36 g) sugar

4 cups (1 kg) San Marzano tomatoes, pureed

3-4 tbsp (34-48 g) Harissa (page 186)

TO FINISH

2 cups (328 g) Cooked Chickpeas (page 204)

8 egg yolks

¼ Preserved Lemon rind (page 196), thinly sliced

¼ cup (10 g) cilantro, coarsely chopped

FOR THE DUCK KEFTA

In a food processor, combine the onion, ginger, garlic, cilantro, vinegar and spices. Pulse to form a paste, scraping the sides of the bowl as needed. Add the breadcrumbs and process until the mixture is combined. In a bowl, combine the ground duck and eggs with the breadcrumb mixture, season with salt and mix together with your hands, making sure not to overmix. Form into 3" (8 cm) balls and press the mixture to ensure that each ball is tight and keeps its shape. Arrange on a parchment-lined sheet pan and refrigerate until you are ready to cook them, up to 24 hours.

Preheat the oven to 350°F (177°C) and bake the kefta until they are just barely cooked and starting to brown, about 15-20 minutes.

FOR THE SWEET & SPICY TOMATO SAUCE

Meanwhile, heat the oil in a large saucepan over moderate heat, then add the onion and garlic and season with salt. Stir and cook over moderate heat until the onions are translucent, about 5 minutes. Add the red wine vinegar and sugar; continue to cook for 3 minutes, stirring often. Add the tomato puree, bring to gentle simmer and continue to cook for 10-15 minutes, or until sauce is thickened. Finish with the harissa, season with salt and adjust with more vinegar and harissa as needed. The sauce should be balanced between sweet, sour and spicy.

TO FINISH

Spoon the cooked chickpeas into a large tagine or round flameproof baking dish with a lid and pour a ½ inch (13 mm) layer of the tomato sauce over them. Arrange the kefta in a circle around the tagine. Cover and simmer over moderate heat for 7-10 minutes, until the kefta are heated through and the sauce is reduced slightly. Arrange the egg yolks around the kefta, cover, and continue to cook for 1 minute over moderate heat. Remove from the heat, and garnish with the preserved lemon and cilantro. To serve, break the egg yolks and stir into the sauce to make it rich and creamy. Serve immediately.

CHEF'S TIP: Ground duck meat can be hard to source; duck breasts will yield the necessary meat-to-fat ratio for this recipe. Your butcher can remove the thick slabs of fat from the breasts and grind the two parts separately to achieve similar results.

Duck Leg Tagine with Saffron and Roasted Olives

This is a fairly straightforward and classic flavor combination from North Africa. Although traditionally it would be prepared with chicken, duck legs have a more robust flavor. Don't panic if you don't have a tagine, you can recreate the dish using another ovenproof clay pot, a Dutch oven or a deep cast-iron casserole. Roasting the olives intensifies their flavor and aroma. Roast some olives and keep them in your fridge for snacking, if nothing else.

4 SERVINGS

Canola oil

4 (8 oz [227 g]) duck legs

Sea salt

2 small yellow onions, thinly sliced

1 large red pepper, thinly sliced

½ cup (68 g) garlic cloves, thinly sliced

¼ cup (28 g) finely grated fresh ginger

2 tsp (4.5 g) Ras El Hanout (page 182)

1 tsp (0.9 g) saffron threads

1 cinnamon stick

2 cups (480 ml) chicken stock or water

12 cilantro sprigs

2 fresh bay leaves

¼ cup (60 ml) Preserved Lemon juice (page 196)

1 cups (188 g) Castelvetrano olives

1 tbsp (15 ml) extra virgin olive oil

1 cups (164 g) Cooked Chickpeas (page 204)

¼ cup (10 g) cilantro, roughly chopped

¼ Preserved Lemon rind (page 196), thinly sliced

In a large, enameled cast-iron skillet or medium casserole, heat a thin layer of canola oil until shimmering. Season the duck legs generously with salt. Place the duck legs, skin-side down, in the skillet and cook over moderate heat until golden brown, about 5 minutes per side. Transfer the duck legs to a plate. Add the onions, pepper, garlic and ginger to the skillet and cook over low heat, stirring occasionally, for about 5 minutes, until the onions start to become translucent. Season with salt and add the ras el hanout, saffron and cinnamon stick; cook for 1 minute, stirring continuously, to bring out the flavor of the spices. Deglaze with a small amount of the stock or water and bring to a boil, about 1–2 minutes, using a wooden spatula to scrape up the browned bits from the bottom of the skillet, then transfer to a tagine. Tie the cilantro sprigs and bay leaves together with kitchen twine to form an herb bundle.

Transfer the duck legs, skin-side up, and any drippings from the plate to the tagine. Add the rest of the stock or water and preserved lemon juice. Bring to a simmer, then cover the tagine and cook over moderate heat for 1–1½ hours, or until the duck legs are very tender.

Meanwhile, preheat the oven to 450°F (232°C). In a small bowl, toss the olives with the olive oil, spread on a parchment-lined baking sheet and roast until the olives are blistered and shrivel slightly, about 15–20 minutes.

Remove and discard the cinnamon stick and herb bundle from the tagine. Combine the roasted olives and cooked chickpeas with the tagine and simmer over moderate to low heat until the sauce is reduced slightly, stirring frequently, about 10–15 minutes. Adjust the seasoning with salt and more lemon juice if needed. Garnish with the cilantro and preserved lemon.

> **CHEF'S TIP:** Although browning the meat before stewing isn't traditional, I like it because it adds another layer of flavor to the dish.
>
> A heat diffuser is always a good idea when you are using a tagine on the stove top.

Greek "Paella"

Inspired by the iconic Spanish dish, this recipe embodies my style of cooking: taking flavors and ingredients that make sense together and pairing them with a cooking technique or recipe that allows for interpretation. The orzo takes the place of the short grain rice, the lamb & fennel sausage stand in for the chorizo and the whole thing is flavored with a light ouzo hint for an anise finish. Add and substitute different varieties of shellfish, as you like.

10 SERVINGS

1 lb (454 g) orzo

2 tbsp (30 ml) extra virgin olive oil, plus more for garnish

8 oz (227 g) Lamb & Fennel Sausage (page 188)

1 tbsp (15 ml) canola oil

1 medium yellow onion, finely diced

½ cup (68 g) garlic cloves, thinly sliced

Sea salt

1 tsp (0.9 g) saffron threads, crushed with fingertips

1 tsp (2.8 g) Spanish sweet smoked paprika

½ tsp chile flakes

2 fresh bay leaves

1 cup (212 g) ½" (13 mm) diced piquillo peppers

1 cup (240 ml) white wine, preferably sauvignon blanc

½ cup (120 ml) ouzo, raki or arak

1 cup (250 g) tomato puree, preferably San Marzano

2 cups (475 ml) Lobster Stock (page 192)

2 cups (268 g) frozen peas

1 lb (454 g) mussels, scrubbed and de-bearded

1 lb (454 g) Manila clams, scrubbed

10 head-on blue prawns, peeled and deveined, head and tail intact

2 tbsp (8 g) roughly chopped flat-leaf parsley

2 tbsp (6.6 g) roughly chopped fresh dill

2 lemons, halved

In a medium pot of boiling salted water, cook the orzo until al dente, about 9 minutes. Drain and rinse well under cold water, shake dry and toss with the olive oil.

Set a 15" (38 cm) stainless steel paella pan, flat skillet or pan over moderate heat. Cook the lamb sausage, breaking it up with a wooden spoon, until some of the fat is rendered and the sausage is browned, about 4 minutes. Add the canola oil, onion and garlic, season with salt and cook over low heat, stirring often, until the onions are translucent and softened, about 8 minutes. Stir in the saffron, paprika and chile flakes; cook for 1 minute, stirring continuously, to bring out the flavor of the spices. Add the bay leaves, piquillo peppers, white wine and ouzo and cook for 10-15 minutes, or until the liquid is reduce by half. Add the tomato puree and lobster stock and bring to a boil. Stir in the peas and cooked orzo, shaking the pan to distribute them evenly. The orzo should be wet but not swimming in liquid; add more stock if necessary. Nestle the mussels, clams and prawns into the orzo, cover the pan with aluminum foil and cook until the mussels and clams are wide open and the prawns are cooked through, about 9-12 minutes. Discard any mussels or clams that fail to open. Garnish with a sprinkling of parsley, dill, a squeeze of lemon juice and a drizzle of olive oil.

Grilled Lamb Chops with Greek Herbs & Spices

When I was growing up, lamb was a staple meat in our house, particularly the tougher cuts, such as the shank or shoulder that needed to be braised or slow cooked. I rarely remember eating the chops. Those always went into the bottom of the pan of grape leaves, to prevent the grape leaves from burning, as they have very little flavor. Nowadays, I must admit that I love a good chop. Cooking meat on the bone really makes a difference in the flavor. The trick to achieving a perfect char on these chops is in slathering them with the rendered lamb fat and the spice blend. I personally prefer to cook lamb chops to medium with a charred outer layer to melt the fat enough to be enjoyable. Serve with Smoky Corn Farina (page 141) or Charred Brussels Sprouts (page 122).

4 SERVINGS AS AN ENTRÉE OR 8 AS A SNACK

FOR THE LAMB CHOPS

1 (4 lb [1.8 kg]) 8-bone whole rack of lamb, domestic preferred, chime bone removed, fat cap trimmed, cut into individual chops (not frenched)

2 tbsp (26 g) rendered lamb fat, warmed but not hot (see Chef's Tip)

2 garlic cloves, sliced

2 fresh oregano sprigs

2 fresh thyme sprigs

Sea salt

Magic Greek Spice (recipe follows), as needed

Extra virgin olive oil

FOR THE MAGIC GREEK SPICE

3¾ tbsp (24 g) black peppercorns

2¼ tsp (5.3 g) dried green peppercorns

2 tsp (2.7 g) coriander seeds

2 tbsp (4.4 g) dried oregano

2½ tsp (7 g) garlic powder

2 tsp (10.4 g) citric acid

FOR THE LAMB CHOPS

In a large, shallow baking pan, liberally brush the chops with the rendered lamb fat, top with half the garlic and herbs, refrigerate until the lamb fat is hard, flip the chops over and repeat on the other side. This can be done up to 1 day in advance. Alternatively, you can skip the lamb fat and just toss the chops in vegetable oil, garlic and herbs and marinate overnight.

Preheat a gas or charcoal grill to moderate-high heat. Bring the chops to room temperature and discard the garlic and herbs. Season liberally with salt and Magic Greek Spice. Grill the chops until firm and charred on the outside, about 3–5 minutes per side, depending on their thickness and how you like the meat done. Rest the meat for 3–5 minutes. Sprinkle more Magic Greek Spice and drizzle with extra virgin olive oil.

FOR THE MAGIC GREEK SPICE

In a small frying pan, combine the black peppercorns, green peppercorns and coriander, and toast over moderate heat, stirring the spices occasionally so they toast evenly, for 2–4 minutes, until they start to warm up and become fragrant. Be careful not to over toast and burn. Remove from the pan and let cool. Pour the spices into a spice grinder and finely grind in small batches; place in a mixing bowl. Grind the oregano, combine with the rest of the ingredients and mix well. Store in an airtight container for up to a month.

CHEF'S TIP: If you don't have access to a charcoal or gas grill, you can achieve similar but less dramatic results by using a ridged cast-iron grill pan. The Magic Greek Spice blend used in this recipe makes more than you will need. But trust me, that's a good thing. It's very versatile and you will want to use it with fish, chicken, beef and vegetables.

To make rendered lamb fat, finely dice the trimmed fat cap or any lamb fat and place in a heavy-bottomed pot with a few tablespoons of water. Slowly melt over moderate heat until the fat is completely rendered, about 1 hour. Reserve in an airtight container in the freezer indefinitely.

Lamb Shanks with Saffron and Pomegranate

Naturally, braised lamb shank is a favorite winter dish for me: sticky-rich gelatinous meat, which when cooked properly—long and slow—falls off the bone. Here we take a Persia-meets-Morocco approach by combining sweet, spicy and tart elements. I've also prepared this dish with oxtail with phenomenal results. Serve alongside Charred Greens (page 125) and Freekeh with Roasted Carrots and Medjool Dates (page 129). And be prepared to be blown away by something you produced with your own hands.

6 SERVINGS

6 lamb foreshanks (6–7 lb [2.7–3.1 kg] total)

Sea salt

Canola oil

6 cups (690 g) coarsely chopped yellow onion

½ cup (74 g) garlic cloves, sliced

¼ cup (28 g) grated fresh ginger

1½ tbsp (10 g) Ras El Hanout (page 182)

2 tsp (1.8 g) saffron threads

1 tsp (2 g) ground ginger

2 tsp (3.2 g) black peppercorns, toasted and ground

6 cups (1.4 L) chicken stock or water

4 cups (960 ml) pomegranate juice

1 tbsp (15 ml) good-quality red wine vinegar

2 tbsp (30 ml) pomegranate molasses

Seeds of 1 medium pomegranate

¼ cup (17 g) cilantro, roughly chopped

¼ cup (31 g) pistachios, chopped

Maldon salt

Preheat the oven to 325°F (163°C). Season the lamb shanks generously with salt. Heat a thin film of the canola oil in a large enameled cast-iron casserole. Working in batches, brown the lamb shanks thoroughly over moderately high heat, turning often, about 3 minutes per side. Transfer the shanks to a baking sheet.

Add the onion, garlic and ginger to the casserole, season with salt and cook over moderate heat, stirring occasionally, for about 5 minutes, until the onions start to become translucent. Add the ras el hanout, saffron, ginger powder and black pepper; cook for 1 minute, stirring continuously, to bring out the flavor of the spices. Deglaze with a small amount of the stock or water and bring to a boil, about 3–5 minutes, using a wooden spatula to scrape up the browned bits from the bottom of the casserole.

Return the lamb and any drippings from the baking sheet to the casserole. Add the rest of the stock or water and pomegranate juice. Bring to a boil, then cover and cook in the preheated oven for 2–3 hours, or until the lamb is very tender. Remove the casserole from the oven.

Carefully transfer the lamb shanks to a baking sheet and cover with foil. Let the cooking liquid stand for 5 minutes, and then skim off the fat that has risen to the top. Simmer the sauce over moderate to low heat until reduced by half, stirring frequently, about 20 minutes. Season the sauce with salt, and add the vinegar and pomegranate molasses. Return the lamb shanks to the sauce and bring to a simmer, while spooning some of the sauce on top of the shanks, until the meat is richly glazed.

Set the lamb shanks on a platter or individual plates, and sprinkle with the pomegranate seeds, cilantro, pistachios and Maldon salt.

North African Spice Roasted Lamb Belly with Creamy Tomato & Cucumber Salad

Mechoui, which is a North African barbecue method, influences this recipe. Lamb belly is fatty and unctuous. It can hold up to big flavors such as this super aggressive rub. The creamy tomato & cucumber salad, although not a traditional accompaniment, is perfect to cut the richness and spiciness of the lamb.

6 SERVINGS

FOR THE LAMB BELLY

½ cup (90 g) kosher salt

½ cup (100 g) sugar

3 tbsp (18 g) cumin seeds, toasted and ground

1 tbsp (8 g) Spanish sweet smoked paprika

2 tsp (3.2 g) black peppercorns, toasted and ground

1 tsp (2 g) cayenne

1 tsp (2.8 g) garlic powder

2 (4–5 lb [1.8–2.3 kg]) lamb bellies

FOR THE CREAMY TOMATO & CUCUMBER SALAD

2 cups (375 g) cherry tomatoes in assorted colors, halved

3 small Lebanese cucumbers, cut into ¼" (6 mm) slices

¼ cup (10 g) cilantro, roughly chopped

1 cup (200 g) Handmade Thick Yogurt (page 189), or Greek yogurt

2 tbsp (30 ml) fresh lemon juice

Sea salt

TO PLATE

1 tbsp Spice Salt made with cumin (page 184)

2 lemons, halved

FOR THE LAMB BELLY

In a small bowl, mix all the dry ingredients for the spice mixture. Generously coat and rub the lamb bellies with the spice mixture and refrigerate for 12–24 hours.

Preheat the oven to 325°F (163°C). Pat the lamb dry with paper towels. Place the lamb snugly, with the fat-side up, in an ovenproof casserole or roasting pan and cook uncovered for 1½–2½ hours, basting with the drippings halfway through, until the meat is fork tender but not falling apart. It should shrink to about half of its original size. Remove the meat from the fat and place on a cutting board for 10–15 minutes to rest. Slice each belly crosswise into 1½ inch (4 cm) pieces and reserve, covered.

FOR THE CREAMY TOMATO & CUCUMBER SALAD

Meanwhile, in a medium bowl, combine all the ingredients for the salad, season with salt and gently mix. Refrigerate for 10–15 minutes to let the flavors combine.

TO PLATE

Sprinkle the lamb belly with the spice salt and a squeeze of fresh lemon. Serve with the creamy tomato & cucumber salad.

CHEF'S TIP: For the spice salt, I like to combine cumin, caraway and coriander for this dish. A simple cumin salt would also work.

Roasted Whole Fish with Fragrant Herb Stuffing

Cooking any meat on the bone makes for an extremely flavorful and moist finished product. This fish preparation is a perfect example. The herb stuffing cooks inside the cavity of the fish, perfuming it with the spices and herbs. Serve with plain basmati rice, Jeweled Rice (page 131) or Spring "Farrotto" (page 142).

4 SERVINGS

2 cups (135 g) cilantro, roughly chopped

2 cups (135 g) flat-leaf parsley, roughly chopped

8 garlic cloves, roughly chopped

6 sun-dried tomato halves, finely chopped

3 tbsp (18 g) cumin seeds, toasted and ground

1 tbsp (8 g) Spanish sweet smoked paprika

1½ tsp (3.6 g) ground Aleppo chile

¼ cup (60 ml) fresh lemon juice

Sea salt

½ cup (120 ml) extra virgin olive oil, plus extra for cooking and garnish

2 (2 lb [907 g]) whole fish, such as snapper, branzini or sea bass, gutted and rinsed

1 lemon, halved

In a food processor, combine the cilantro, parsley, garlic, sun-dried tomatoes, ground cumin, paprika, Aleppo chile and lemon juice. Season with salt and pulse to form a paste, scraping the sides of the bowl as needed, and slowly drizzle in the olive oil.

Preheat the oven to 425°F (218°C) and line a large, rimmed baking sheet with parchment paper. Meanwhile, place the fish on a cutting board and use kitchen shears to cut and discard the fins. With a very sharp knife, cut four, 2" (5 cm)-long, ¼" (6 mm)-deep slits into both sides of the fish.

Rub both fish all over with the olive oil; season generously with salt and rub a small amount of the stuffing on the outside of the fish, making sure to get into the slits. Stuff the cavities with the herb stuffing and set the fish on the baking sheet. Roast for about 30 minutes, until cooked through.

Transfer the fish to a platter. Squeeze the lemon over the fish and drizzle with a little more olive oil.

CHEF'S TIP: The slits allow the herb stuffing to penetrate into the flesh of the fish.

Roasted Chicken with Sumac and Onions

Who doesn't love a roasted chicken? I'm very leery of people that don't love roasted chicken, vegetarians excluded. To me it's a comfort dish that sees no boundaries; no matter what part of the world you grew up in, rich or poor, everyone eats roasted chicken. This recipe takes the humble protein to a whole new level of delicious, combining it with aromatic spices and a lemony finish.

6 SERVINGS

3 tbsp (26.1 g) ground sumac

2 tsp (8 g) whole allspice, toasted and ground

2 tsp (2.7 g) coriander seeds, toasted and ground

3 cardamom pods, ground

½ tsp (0.5 g) saffron threads, crushed

1 tsp (2.8 g) grated nutmeg

½ tsp (1.3 g) ground cinnamon

1 (3 lb [1.4kg]) whole chicken, cut into 8 pieces, or same weight in skin-on, bone-in chicken thighs

Sea salt

Olive oil

12 garlic cloves, peeled

3 medium red onions, cut into 8 wedges

¼ cup (60 ml) fresh lemon juice

Extra virgin olive oil

In a large bowl, combine the spices and rub with your fingertips. Reserve half of the spices and add the chicken to the bowl, toss and season with salt and a drizzle of olive oil, and marinate for at least 2 hours or up to overnight.

Preheat the oven to 350°F (177°C). In a large, enameled cast-iron skillet or medium flameproof casserole, heat a thin film of olive oil until shimmering. Add the garlic cloves and onion wedges, season with salt and continue to cook for 4 minutes over high heat, until the garlic and onion are lightly browned. Stir in the reserved spices. Nestle the marinated chicken, skin-side up, in the skillet. Transfer the skillet to the oven and roast, uncovered, for about 50 minutes, until the chicken is very tender and the onions are melted. Remove from the oven, add the lemon juice and stir well. Adjust the seasoning with salt if need, let rest for a few minutes and drizzle with some extra virgin olive oil.

CHEF'S TIP: Sumac is a magical ingredient. It lends a brick red hue to anything that it touches and gives foods a bright, tart finish.

Spring Lamb "Cassoulet"

You know that really hearty, rich, slow-cooked casserole from the south of France? Well this is a lighter, more modern version that highlights lamb meat rather than pork and duck. Light yet complex and very flavorful, this cooks in half the time as a traditional cassoulet.

8 SERVINGS

FOR THE SPRING VEGETABLE CASSOULET

1½ cups (200 g) dried cannellini beans, soaked overnight, drained

Sea salt

4 lb (1.8 kg) fresh shelling beans and peas (such as cranberry, edamame, young fava, fresh chickpeas and English peas), shelled

1 lb (454 g) assorted pole beans (Romano, yellow and purple wax and Dragon Tongue)

2 tbsp (30 ml) canola oil

1 small onion, finely diced

2 carrots, peeled and finely diced

8 oz (227 g) Lamb & Fennel Sausage (page 188)

1 oz (28 g) dried porcini mushrooms, soaked in hot water for 15 minutes

1 cup (165 g) Roasted Tomatoes (page 204)

4 cups (960 ml) Rich Lamb Stock (page 194)

FOR THE LAMB LOIN

1 tsp (2.7 g) Spanish sweet smoked paprika

2 tbsp (30 ml) canola oil

2 (12–16 oz [340–454 g]) boneless lamb loins, trimmed

TO FINISH

2 tbsp (28 g) unsalted butter

1 cup (64 g) panko breadcrumbs

Sea salt

Micro beet greens or other small greens, for garnish

FOR THE SPRING VEGETABLE CASSOULET

Place the cannellini beans in a medium saucepan, cover by 2 inches (5 cm) of water and bring to a boil. Simmer over low heat, stirring occasionally, until the beans are just tender, about 1½–2 hours, adding more water as needed to keep the beans covered by 2 inches (5 cm). Season the cooked beans with a generous amount of salt and refrigerate for 1 hour or up to 3 days.

Fill 2 large bowls halfway with ice. In a medium saucepan of salted boiling water, cook the shelling beans and peas until they start to soften, about 2–3 minutes. Pour the cooking liquid and the beans and peas into the ice bowl to cool completely. Drain and pat dry with a paper towel.

In a large saucepan of salted boiling water, cook the pole beans until they are tender but still crisp, about 2 minutes. Pour the cooking liquid and the beans into the second ice bowl to cool completly. Drain and pat dry with a paper towel.

Meanwhile, in a large skillet, heat the canola oil until shimmering. Add the onions and carrots, season with salt and cook over moderate heat, stirring occasionally, until the onions are softened, about 3 minutes. Add the lamb sausage, breaking it up with a wooden spoon and cook until some of the fat is rendered and the sausage is browned, about 4 minutes. Strain and reserve the liquid from the mushrooms. Add the mushrooms and roasted tomatoes to the pan and combine. Add the lamb stock and reserved mushroom liquid and simmer over moderate heat until the sauce reduces by half and starts to thicken, about 8-10 minutes. Stir in the cooked cannellini beans, shelling beans, peas and pole beans until warmed through. Season with salt and reserve warm.

FOR THE LAMB LOIN

In a large bowl, combine the smoked paprika and 1 tablespoon (15 ml) of the oil. Then add the lamb loins and turn to coat. Let marinate in the refrigerator for a minimum of 1 hour and up to overnight.

Preheat the oven to 400°F (205°C). In a large cast-iron skillet, heat the remaining canola oil over moderately high heat. Place the lamb loins in the skillet and sear for 2 minutes, turn and continue to cook for about 2 minutes. Transfer the skillet to the oven and roast the loins to the desired doneness, about 7-8 minutes for medium-rare. Remove pan from oven and place the loins on a cutting board; rest the meat for 5 minutes. Slice crosswise, against the grain, into ½ inch (13 mm) slices and reserve warm.

TO FINISH

Meanwhile, in a large skillet, heat the butter until it starts to bubble, add the breadcrumbs and cook over moderate heat, stirring continuously, until they are toasted and have a deep golden color, about 4-5 minutes. Season with salt.

Mound the vegetable cassoulet onto a serving platter and arrange the sliced lamb loin on top. Garnish with the toasted breadcrumbs and micro beet greens.

Steamed Clams with Arak

I love simply steamed clams with a little butter and some crusty bread. Anise and shellfish are a great combination that I also love. Here, the clams get a triple dose of anise, in the forms of fresh fennel, arak and dill. This makes a great snack, but if you are in the mood for something more substantial, add some cooked orzo from the Greek "Paella" recipe (page 101) at the end, and garnish with crumbled feta.

4 SERVINGS

3 lb (1.36 kg) Manila clams

1 tbsp (15 ml) canola oil

1 medium shallot, finely minced

1 medium fennel bulb, trimmed and cut into thin slices, lengthwise

Sea salt

3 tbsp (45 ml) arak, ouzo or other anise-flavored liquor

¼ cup (60 ml) vegetable stock, dry white wine or water

3 tbsp (85 g) unsalted butter, diced and chilled

1 tbsp (3.4 g) fresh dill, roughly chopped, plus more for garnish

A pinch of chile flakes

1 lemon, halved

Crusty bread, to serve

Scrub the clams clean under cold running water with a brush. Discard any clams that don't close after a small tap. Heat a large saucepan over moderate heat; add the canola oil, shallots and fennel. Season with salt and cook for 2-4 minutes, until the shallots become translucent. Add the clams, arak and vegetable stock and season with salt. Cover, turn the heat up to high and steam the clams, shaking the pan occasionally until the clams open, about 5 minutes. While the sauce is simmering, slowly add the butter to the pan and swirl in the dill, chile flakes and a squeeze of lemon. Adjust the seasoning with salt if necessary.

Place in a serving bowl and garnish with the reserved dill. Serve immediately with crusty bread.

CHEF'S TIP: Discard any clams that don't open after steaming.

Spice-Crusted Beef Strip Loin

This recipe is inspired by *steak au poivre*, or pepper steak. Here the steak gets a crusting of coarsely crushed coriander, cumin, black peppercorns, fennel and caraway before being seared in a hot pan with butter and garlic. If you are looking for a simple and quick recipe that is great way to update the boring old steak, you've found it.

2 SERVINGS

FOR THE PRESERVED LEMON YOGURT

½ cup (100 g) Homemade Thick Yogurt (page 189), or Greek yogurt

1 tbsp (15 ml) Preserved Lemon juice (page 196)

¼ Preserved Lemon rind (page 196), finely minced

1 tbsp (4 g) flat-leaf parsley, finely chopped

Pinch of cayenne

Sea salt

FOR THE SPICE-CRUSTED STEAK

1 tbsp (7.7 g) black peppercorns

2 tbsp (8 g) coriander seeds

1 tbsp (6 g) cumin seeds

1 tbsp (7.5 g) caraway seeds

1 tbsp (6 g) fennel seeds

2 (12 oz [340 g]) pieces of thick-cut beef strip loin or rib eye

Canola oil

Sea salt

2 tbsp (28 g) unsalted butter, diced

3 garlic cloves, not peeled, crushed

2 fresh thyme sprigs

Maldon salt

FOR THE PRESERVED LEMON YOGURT

In a small bowl, combine all of the ingredients, season with salt and whisk to combine.

FOR THE SPICE-CRUSTED STEAK

Crush the black peppercorn in a mortar, then place in a bowl. Combine the rest of the spices and crush or coarsely grind in a spice grinder or mortar. Add to the bowl with the black pepper and store in an airtight container for up to 30 days, as this makes more than what you will need in the recipe.

Bring the steaks to room temperature. Brush with canola oil and season liberally with sea salt. Spread a thin layer of the spice mixture on a plate and place the steak on top; crust on one side with the spice blend.

Meanwhile, heat a cast-iron skillet over high heat and add a thin layer of canola oil. Place the steaks in the skillet with the spice side down, and cook for 2-3 minutes, until the spices become aromatic and the steak starts to brown, then turn and continue to cook for about 2-3 minutes. Lower the temperature to moderate low heat and add the butter, garlic and thyme. Tip the pan and spoon the melted butter over the steaks and continue to cook the steaks until firm and charred on the outside, about 2-5 minutes, depending on their thickness and how you like the meat done. Place the steaks on a cutting board; rest for 5-8 minutes. Slice the steaks crosswise into ½ inch (13 mm) slices. Arrange the steak on a large platter or individual plates. Season with the crunchy salt and serve with the preserved lemon yogurt on the side.

CHEF'S TIP: The spices are not pre-toasted here because they get toasted as they cook in the pan with the steak.

Salmon & Clam Tagine

This dish has been on the menu at Saffron for many years. Every year when wild salmon comes into season, we have to feature it. We cook the salmon in the traditional tagine vessel, but it could be prepared in a deep-sided pan or cast-iron casserole, fitted with a lid. The charmoula perfumes the fish as it slow cooks, making for a perfectly spiced and cooked piece of fish that just melts in your mouth. Serve with crusty bread to dip in the sauce.

4 SERVINGS

4 (5 oz [142 g]) pieces king salmon or other wild salmon, pin bones removed, skinned

¼ cup (59 g) plus 2 tbsp (29.5 g) Charmoula (page 177)

Canola oil

1 medium fennel bulb, cored and sliced

1 large red pepper, sliced

3 garlic cloves, thinly sliced

Sea salt

3 cups (750 g) San Marzano tomatoes and juice, crushed by hand

½ cup (94 g) Picholine olives, plus 2 tbsp (30 ml) olive juice

1 tbsp (18 g) Preserved Lemon "Plazma" (page 199)

2 tbsp (30 ml) fresh lemon juice

12 assorted fingerling potatoes, scrubbed, not peeled

20 Manila clams, washed and scrubbed

2 tbsp (28 g) unsalted butter, diced

2 tbsp (8 g) flat-leaf parsley, roughly chopped

¼ Preserved Lemon rind (page 196), thinly sliced

Marinate the salmon in the 2 tablespoons (29.5 g) of charmoula for a minimum of 2 hours and up to 24 hours.

Heat a thin film of canola oil in a large tagine or cast-iron casserole, add the fennel, and cook over moderate-high heat until the fennel starts to brown, about 6 minutes, stirring often. Add the red pepper and garlic, and season with salt; continue to cook for 3 minutes, stirring often. Add the crushed tomatoes, bring to a gentle simmer and continue to cook for 10 minutes, or until the sauce is slightly thickened. Stir in the remaining charmoula, olives, olive juice, preserved lemon "plazma," and lemon juice and adjust the seasoning with salt.

Meanwhile, in a medium saucepot, combine the potatoes with 3 tablespoons (25.2 g) salt, cover with water and bring to a boil. Reduce the heat and simmer the potatoes, uncovered, until tender, about 10–15 minutes. Check by inserting a paring knife into the center of the potatoes. Drain the liquid and add the potatoes to the tagine.

Season the marinated salmon with salt and nestle in the sauce along with the clams and butter. Cover and cook over moderate heat for 5–10 minutes, depending on the thickness of the fish fillet and your desired doneness of the fish. (I prefer medium.) Remove from the heat and let steam for 2 minutes; remove and discard any clams that didn't open up. Garnish with the parsley and preserved lemon slices.

CHEF'S TIP: I don't typically follow rules, but this one makes sense to me. Tagines should never be served with a side of couscous. In North African cuisine, couscous is a big deal; it's a celebratory dish that is always the center of the meal, not a side dish.

Stuffed Eggplant with Lamb and Tomato

This recipe was adapted from the book that my parents wrote but never published in the late 1980s. The book included an entire chapter that was devoted to stuffed vegetables. This recipe recalled a memory of living in Jordan and coming home from school and having this for lunch. I remember walking into the house to the aromas of dark spices and toasted pine nuts. It was typically served with basmati rice, marinated olives and assorted pickled vegetables.

6 SERVINGS

3 large eggplants, halved

Olive oil

Sea salt

2 small onions, finely chopped

4 garlic cloves, made into a paste

1½ lb (680 g) ground lamb, preferably from the shoulder

2 tsp (4.4 g) whole cloves, ground

1 tsp (2.6 g) ground cinnamon

1 tsp (1.4 g) chili flakes

1 tsp (2.4 g) ground cardamom pods

1 tsp (2.5 g) black peppercorns, toasted and ground

½ cup (118 g) pine nuts, fried (page 205), plus more for garnish

3 cups (750 g) San Marzano tomatoes, crushed by hand

2 tsp (9 g) sugar

¼ cup (17 g) flat-leaf parley, roughly chopped

Preheat the oven to 425°F (218°C). Arrange the eggplants in a large baking dish, cut-sides up. Brush with olive oil and season with salt. Bake for about 20 minutes, until the skin is browned and the flesh starts becoming soft. Split the eggplant down the middle, making sure not to tear the skin on the bottom.

In a large skillet, heat 1 tablespoon (15 ml) olive oil. Add the onion and garlic, season with salt and cook over moderate heat, stirring often, until softened, about 8 minutes. Add the ground lamb and the spices. Cook, breaking up the meat with a wooden spoon, for about 4 minutes, or until the meat is cooked through. Stir in the pine nuts, crushed tomatoes and sugar; season with salt.

Reduce the oven temperature to 350°F (177°C). Spoon the lamb mixture onto the split eggplants in the baking dish. Cover the dish with foil and bake for about 30–40 minutes, until the eggplant is very tender.

Transfer the eggplants to individual plates or a platter and garnish with the parsley and reserved pine nuts.

Whole Fried Fish with Traditional Middle Eastern Accompaniments

One of my earliest real cooking memories was making this recipe with my father after he came back from fishing in the Persian Gulf. I love the scent of garam masala. Its flavor works especially well with fish, without overpowering it. The accompaniments used here are three distinct flavors: creamy and slightly spicy tahini sauce, a sour and refreshing tomato salad and a spiced herbaceous cilantro sauce.

4 SERVINGS

FOR THE TAHINI SAUCE

1 cup (230 g) tahini

1 tsp (4 g) Homemade Thick Yogurt (page 189), or Greek yogurt

3 tbsp (12 g) flat-leaf parsley, finely chopped

3 tbsp (12 g) cilantro, finely chopped

1 garlic clove, finely grated

¼ cup (60 ml) fresh lemon juice

¼ small jalapeño, seeded and finely diced

Sea salt

About ½ cup (120 ml) water

FOR THE TOMATO & CUCUMBER SALAD

1½ lb (680 g) mixed heirloom and cherry tomatoes, cut into wedges

2 small Lebanese cucumbers, cut into ¼" (6 mm) slices

¼ small yellow onion, thinly sliced

¼ cup (6 g) flat-leaf parsley, leaves only

1 tsp (2.9 g) ground sumac

1 tsp (5 ml) extra virgin olive oil

Sea salt

FOR THE SPICY CILANTRO SAUCE

1½ cups (100 g) cilantro, roughly chopped

3 sun-dried tomato halves, finely chopped

1½ tbsp (9 g) cumin seeds, toasted and ground

1 tsp (2.7 g) Spanish sweet smoked paprika

½ tsp (1.2 g) ground Aleppo chile

3 tbsp (45 ml) fresh lemon juice

¼ cup (60 ml) extra virgin olive oil

FOR THE FISH

⅓ cup (79 ml) fresh lemon juice

4 garlic cloves, finely grated

3 tbsp (25.2 g) plus 1 tbsp (8.4 g) Garam Masala (page 181)

2 (1½–2 lb [680–907 g]) pieces of whole fish, such as branzini, snapper or bass, scaled, gutted and rinsed

Canola oil, for deep frying

2 cups (250 g) all-purpose flour

2 tbsp (16.8 g) sea salt, plus more for seasoning

FOR THE TAHINI SAUCE

In a small bowl, combine all the ingredients for the sauce, season with salt and whisk, adding a thin stream of water to make into a thick, honey consistency. Refrigerate for 10–15 minutes to let the flavors meld. Can be made up to 4 hours ahead.

FOR THE TOMATO & CUCUMBER SALAD

In a medium bowl, combine all the ingredients for the salad, season with salt and gently toss. Refrigerate for 10–15 minutes to let the flavors combine.

FOR THE SPICY CILANTRO SAUCE

In a small food processor, combine all the ingredients, excluding the olive oil. Pulse to a chunky paste, then slowly drizzle in the olive oil to emulsify. Refrigerate for 10–15 minutes to let the flavors meld. Can be made up to 4 hours ahead.

FOR THE FISH

Mix the lemon juice, garlic and 3 tablespoons (25.2 g) of the garam masala in a small bowl. Place the fish on a cutting board, and, with a very sharp knife, cut four 2" (5 cm)-long, ¼ inch (6 mm)-deep slits into both sides of the fish. Rub the spice mixture on both sides of the fish and into the cavities; marinate for 30–60 minutes.

In a large, heavy pot no more than half filled with oil, or a deep fryer, heat the oil to 350°F (177°C). Meanwhile, mix the flour, remaining 1 tablespoon (8.4 g) garam masala and 2 tablespoons (30 g)of salt in a large, shallow bowl. Season the fish liberally with salt. Place the fish in the mixing bowl and evenly dust the whole fish in the mixture and shake to rid of excess flour. Transfer to a plate and let stand for 10 minutes. Carefully lower the fish into the oil and fry until brown, about 7–12 minutes. Remove from the oil and drain briefly on absorbent towels. Season with salt and serve immediately with the accompaniments.

Swordfish with Smoked Hazelnut Romesco & Grilled Spring Onions

This Spanish-influenced recipe pays homage to the famous Catalan preparation of *calçots*, a variety of scallion that has a mild onion flavor. If you can get your hands on *calçots*, by all means, use them. I substitute grilled onions and serve it with the iconic romesco sauce, which is prefect with fish and vegetables. I believe that swordfish is better when it's not cooked all the way through, but that is a matter of personal taste.

4 SERVINGS

FOR THE SMOKED HAZELNUT ROMESCO

½ cup (68 g) hazelnuts, toasted and chopped (see page 205)

½ cup (106 g) piquillo peppers, drained, chopped

2 San Marzano tomatoes, crushed

2 garlic cloves, chopped

1 tbsp (8 g) Spanish sweet smoked paprika

¼ tsp cayenne

2 tsp (10 ml) good-quality sherry vinegar

1 tsp (5 ml) fresh lemon juice

Sea salt

¼ cup (60 ml) extra virgin olive oil, plus extra for garnish

FOR THE SWORDFISH & SPRING ONIONS

8 spring onions, bulbs cut in half

Canola oil

Sea salt

4 (6 oz [170 g]) swordfish steaks, at least 1" (3 cm) thick

1 lemon, halved

FOR THE SMOKED HAZELNUT ROMESCO

In a food processor, combine all of the ingredients, except the oil, season with salt and pulse to form a paste, scraping the sides of the bowl as needed, and then slowly drizzle in the olive oil. The romesco should be a little chunky. Refrigerate extra romesco in an airtight container for up to a week.

FOR THE SWORDFISH & SPRING ONIONS

Preheat a gas or charcoal grill to moderate-high heat.

Toss the spring onions in a medium bowl with canola oil and season with salt. Place the cut side on the grill and cook for 3–5 minutes, until the edges start to char. Flip and continue to cook for 3–4 minutes.

Lightly brush the swordfish steaks with canola oil and season with salt.

Generously oil the grill with canola oil to prevent the fish from sticking. Grill the swordfish for 3 minutes per side, until nicely browned outside and just white throughout. Rest for 2 minutes and squeeze the lemon on top of the fish.

Spoon some of the romesco onto 4 individual plates, place the swordfish on top of the romesco and garnish with the grilled spring onions, more of the romesco and a drizzle of olive oil.

CHEF'S TIP: You can substitute almonds for the hazelnuts in the romesco if you are in a pinch.

Whole Roasted Lamb Shoulder with Arabic Spices

One of my favorite dishes growing up was my mother's roasted leg of lamb. I remember a heavy clove, cardamom and allspice aroma wafting through the house as she prepared it. In my opinion, when talking about roasting lamb, the shoulder is the best meat for the job because of the high fat content, which keeps it moist and juicy. In this recipe, the lamb is marinated overnight in a yogurt marinade that is flavored with dark spices and slowly cooked for close to 5 hours at a low temperature, resulting in extremely tender meat. I often joke that if you look at the meat long enough, it will fall apart. For a classic combination, serve alongside Jeweled Rice (page 131).

6–8 SERVINGS

½ cup (58 g) plus 1 tbsp (7.3 g) Se7en Spice (page 184)

2 tbsp (13.2 g) whole cloves, toasted and ground

2 tsp (5 g) black peppercorns, toasted and ground

3 tbsp (39 g) Homemade Thick Yogurt (page 189), or Greek yogurt

6 tbsp (90 ml) fresh lemon juice

8 garlic cloves

½ small yellow onion, roughly chopped

1 (3-4 lb [1.4-1.8 kg]) boneless lamb shoulder, fat cap trimmed and patted dry

3 tbsp (45 ml) canola oil

Sea salt

In a food processor or blender, combine ½ cup (58 g) of the se7en spice, cloves, black pepper, yogurt, 2 tablespoons (30 ml) of the lemon juice, garlic and onion. Process until you have a very smooth paste. Generously coat and rub the lamb with the marinade and refrigerate for 6-24 hours.

Preheat the oven to 325°F (163°C). Bring the lamb shoulder to room temperature, rub it with oil and the remaining 1 tablespoon (7.3 g) se7en spice and generously season with salt. Place the lamb with the fat side up in an ovenproof casserole or roasting pan, cover with foil and cook for 2½-3½ hours. Remove the foil and continue cooking for 1½-2 hours, basting with the drippings regularly, until the meat is well browned and fork tender. Remove from the oven and let the lamb rest, lightly covered in foil, for 20-30 minutes.

Carefully remove the meat from the pot and place on a serving platter. Pour the roasting liquid into a container, let stand for 5 minutes and then skim off the fat that has risen to the top. Drizzle the reserved roasting liquid and the remaining 4 tablespoons (60 ml) lemon juice over the meat and serve.

CHEF'S TIP: Don't remove all of the fat cap; leave a thin layer. As the meat roasts, the fat renders and naturally bastes the meat.

Side Dishes

In the eastern Mediterranean, rice, grains and pulses are a part of every meal and are typically served at the center of the plate. As in many cultures, these starches augment the meal.

In this chapter, I have taken a Western approach to side dishes and included recipes that can accompany large plates to compose a full meal. Alternatively, they can be served as appetizers, mezze or a vegetarian meal.

Charred Brussels Sprouts with Spicy Anchovy Butter

Use this recipe as a blueprint for infinite possibilities with many vegetables. The main technique here is to char the vegetable in a small amount of oil and introduce a more robust flavor. Use your favorite vegetables: cauliflower, okra, green beans and artichokes all work wonderfully. The anchovy butter is inspired by flavors of *bagna cauda*, the Piedmontese "hot bath" sauce. This recipe makes an appearance on the menu at Saffron on a yearly basis. It's a crowd favorite, even for those who aren't big fans of anchovies.

4–6 SERVINGS

FOR THE SPICY ANCHOVY BUTTER

3 oz (85 g) best-quality anchovy fillet in oil, rinsed

1 cup (67 g) flat-leaf parsley, roughly chopped

1 tsp (1.4 g) chile flakes

¼ lb (113 g) unsalted butter

1 garlic clove, finely grated

FOR THE BRUSSELS SPROUTS

Sea salt

½ tsp (2 g) baking soda

1½ lb (680 g) brussels sprouts

½ cup (120 ml) canola oil

2 tbsp (30 ml) fresh lemon juice

2 tbsp (6 g) finely chopped chives

FOR THE SPICY ANCHOVY BUTTER

Place all the ingredients in a food processor; puree until smooth and reserve. This makes more than is needed in the recipe, but can be frozen for up to a month.

FOR THE BRUSSELS SPROUTS

Fill a large bowl with salted ice water. Bring a large pot with about 3 quarts (2.8 L) of water to a boil. Add the baking soda and enough salt to make the water salty like the sea.

Meanwhile, remove the outer leaves of the brussels sprouts. Trim the ends off and split in half lengthwise. Carefully drop the brussels sprouts into the boiling water and cook until tender, about 3 minutes. Drain immediately and immerse in the salted ice water to cool completely. Drain and pat dry with a paper towel. This can be done up to 1 day in advance.

In a large frying pan, heat the oil until it starts to smoke. Cook the brussels sprouts, cut-side down, undisturbed, for 2–4 minutes, until they start to brown. Flip the brussels sprouts and add the spicy anchovy butter; lower the heat to moderate and continue to cook until the butter melts, stirring occasionally. Season the brussels sprouts with salt and finish with the lemon juice and chives.

CHEF'S TIP: Baking soda helps maintain the beautiful vibrant color of green vegetables. Be careful, though, because too much baking soda will turn the vegetables mushy.

Charred Cauliflower with Cumin, Paprika and Feta

Charring vegetables in a hot pan gives them a complex flavor that is very popular in the Levant, similar to stir-frying in Asian cuisine. Cauliflower is great at soaking up flavors. Here it's paired with lemony and spicy flavors as well as with creamy feta.

6–8 SERVINGS

Canola oil

1 head (1½ lb [660 g]) cauliflower, halved, cored and cut into 1" (3 cm) florets

Sea salt

1 tbsp (6 g) cumin seeds, toasted and ground

Pinch of chile flakes

2 garlic cloves, finely grated

3 tbsp (45 ml) fresh lemon juice

¼ cup (40 g) crumbled cow's milk feta

2 tbsp (8 g) flat-leaf parsley, roughly chopped

Spanish sweet smoked paprika, for garnish

Extra virgin olive oil, for garnish

Heat a thin film of canola oil in a large frying pan over high heat until it starts to smoke. Working in batches, cook the cauliflower florets until they start to brown and blister, about 2 minutes. Shake the pan around and add a small amount of oil if the cauliflower absorbed what was in the pan. Season with salt and continue to cook over moderate heat until the cauliflower is evenly charred and slightly soft, shaking the pan often. Add the cumin, chile flakes, garlic and lemon juice. Cook for 30 seconds, stirring the whole time. Place the cauliflower in a serving dish and garnish with the feta, parsley, a dusting of paprika and a generous drizzle of olive oil.

Charred Greens with Aleppo Chile and Lemon

Cooked leafy greens are a staple in the Levant, typically served at room temperature or even slightly chilled. Here, I cook the greens quickly in a very hot pan with extra virgin olive oil and serve them warm. I like to combine an assortment of greens and herbs to achieve a balance of bitter, spicy and sour. Serve them as a part of a mezze spread or as a side dish with pretty much any recipe in this book. If you have leftovers, chop them up and warm them slowly in some water and serve them with fresh pita as a dip.

4–6 SERVINGS

¼ cup (60 ml) extra virgin olive oil, plus extra for garnishing

2 lb (908 g) assorted greens (baby kale, baby spinach, frisee, baby arugula, Swiss chard), washed, dried and roughly chopped

Sea salt

½ cup (27 g) fresh dill leaves, roughly chopped, plus a few leaves for garnishing

¼ cup (17 g) flat-leaf parsley leaves, roughly chopped

1 tsp (2.4 g) ground Aleppo chile, plus extra for garnishing

4 tbsp (60 ml) fresh lemon juice

Working in 2 batches, heat a large skillet and add half of the olive oil; heat over high heat until it starts to smoke. Add the greens and season with salt. Cook, stirring often, until softened, about 4–6 minutes. Add the dill, parsley, Aleppo chile and lemon juice. Continue to cook over high heat, shaking the pan often, until most of the liquid has evaporated, about 2 minutes. Taste and adjust the seasoning with salt. Transfer to a serving bowl, garnish with a sprinkling of Aleppo chile, a few leaves of dill and a drizzling of olive oil. Serve immediately.

CHEF'S TIP: You can play around with the combination of greens as you like. In the summertime, I like to use dandelion greens with wild arugula and purslane.

Coriander Potatoes with Roasted Tomatoes and Caramelized Paprika Butter

Coriander seed is one of my favorite spices. Its sweet, lemony flavor is perfect in toning down pungent spices in spice blends. And it's great on its own, as it adds an orange-like perfume to anything that it's combined with. Here, the seeds, along with the leaves (cilantro) of the plant—which taste nothing alike—are used to harmonize each other's flavors. I've been serving this recipe at Saffron for several years. Guests seem to never tire of it, and neither do I. It's a perfect match to the Spice-Crusted Beef Strip Loin (page 113) or the Braised Veal Breast (page 95).

6 SERVINGS

FOR THE POTATOES

2 lb (908 g) assorted fingerling potatoes, scrubbed, not peeled

2 tbsp (18 g) sea salt

3 sprigs of thyme

2 tbsp (30 ml) canola oil

3 tbsp (12 g) coriander seeds, lightly crushed

2 cups (300 g) assorted color cherry or grape tomatoes, halved

TO FINISH

1 cup (200 g) Homemade Thick Yogurt (page 189), or Greek yogurt

1 garlic clove, finely grated

1 tbsp (15 ml) fresh lemon juice

Sea salt

½ cup (87 g) Caramelized Paprika Butter (page 176), warmed

Micro cilantro or very small leaves of cilantro, for garnish

FOR THE POTATOES

In a medium pot, combine the potatoes, salt and thyme, barely cover with water and bring to a boil over high heat. Reduce the heat and simmer the potatoes, uncovered, until tender, about 15-18 minutes. Check by inserting a paring knife in the center of the potatoes. Drain the liquid and let cool at room temperature. Once the potatoes are cool enough to handle, discard the thyme, then lightly crush with the palm of your hand.

Meanwhile, preheat the oven to 450°F (232°C). Heat the canola oil in a large ovenproof skillet over moderate-high heat. Add the crushed potatoes and cook, undisturbed, for 1 minute. Toss in the coriander and cherry tomatoes. Place the skillet in the oven and cook for 5-7 minutes, or until the tomatoes start to brown on the edges and the potatoes are warmed through and starting to brown. Remove from the oven and reserve warm.

TO FINISH

In a small mixing bowl, combine the yogurt, garlic and lemon juice, season with salt and whisk to combine. Equally divide and spread the yogurt with the back of a spoon among 6 individual bowls. Spoon the potatoes in the center of the bowls. Drizzle the caramelized paprika butter on and around the potatoes and garnish with a few leaves of micro cilantro.

Eggplant Lovash with Tahini Yogurt

There were two inspirations for this recipe. The first was the popular Turkish dish *imam bayildi*, in which whole eggplants are stuffed with onion and tomatoes and stewed with lots of olive oil. The other was *musakhan*, which is an iconic Palestinian dish of sumac-stewed onions that are wrapped in *markook*, or lovash bread. Here, all of the ingredients are chopped into smaller pieces and stewed in olive oil. This is the best thing ever with the Roasted Chicken (page 108). The eggplant stew makes a great mezze on its own, sprinkled with parsley, mint and a little pomegranate molasses.

8 SERVINGS

FOR THE EGGPLANT STEW & LOVASH ROLLS

1 large eggplant, cut into 1" (3 cm) cubes

1 tbsp (8.4 g) sea salt, plus more for seasoning

1 small yellow onion, halved and cut into ¼" (6 mm) slices

1½ cups (375 g) San Marzano tomatoes, drained and crushed by hand

4 garlic cloves, peeled

1 tbsp (3 g) fresh thyme, roughly chopped

½ tsp (1.3 g) black peppercorns, toasted and ground

1½ cups (360 ml) extra virgin olive oil, plus more for garnish

1½ cups (360 ml) canola oil

2–3 (roughly 24" [60 cm] diameter) thin lovash, taboon or markook bread

TO SERVE

1 cup (216 g) Tahini Yogurt (page 202)

Ground sumac, for garnish

FOR THE EGGPLANT STEW

Place the eggplant in a large bowl and sprinkle with 1 tablespoon (8.4 g) of salt. Set aside for 30–60 minutes. Gently squeeze the eggplant to extract the liquid, then pat dry with a paper towel.

Preheat the oven to 300°F (150°C). In a small enameled cast-iron casserole, combine the eggplant, onion, tomatoes, garlic and thyme, season with black pepper and a few pinches of salt and cover with the olive and canola oils. Cover the casserole tightly with foil and transfer to the oven. Cook for 2½–3½ hours, until the eggplant is very tender. Let cool completely in the oil. This can be made up to 1 week in advance.

FOR THE LOVASH ROLLS

Preheat the oven to 400°F (205°C). Strain the eggplant from the oil, reserving the oil for future use. Spread the lovash on a work surface and spoon the eggplant stew in the middle of the lovash in a horizontal line from the right to the left side. Fold the bread over the eggplant and roll into a log. Cut the roll into 4 equal-size pieces; repeat with the other pieces of lovash. Place on a parchment-lined baking pan, then brush with some of the olive oil, sprinkle with salt and bake for 8–10 minutes, until the tops of the lovash rolls are brown and crispy.

TO SERVE

Divide the tahini yogurt among 6 individual plates. Place the lovash roll adjacent to the sauce, sprinkle with sumac and lightly drizzle with olive oil.

CHEF'S TIP: Reuse the cooking oil for more flavor. Just keep adding fresh oil to get the desired amount.

Freekeh with Roasted Carrots and Medjool Dates

Freekeh is charred green wheat that is very popular in the Levant, especially in Egyptian and Palestinian cuisines, where it's typically prepared with poultry. I grew up eating freekeh soup and freekeh pilaf with roasted or poached chicken, favorites of mine. In this recipe, the freekeh is served with roasted carrots, which play beautifully with the smoky, chewy characteristics of the freekeh and the spicy notes of the harissa-laced yogurt. The cooking method is similar to cooking rice pilaf, but with a longer "rest" time for the water to absorb into the grain.

4–6 SERVINGS

FOR THE FREEKEH

2 cups (320 g) freekeh, washed and soaked in water for 10 minutes

2 tbsp (30 ml) olive oil

3 cups (710 ml) vegetable stock or water

Sea salt

FOR THE CARROTS

6-8 heirloom carrots, tops trimmed, scrubbed with a brush under water and cut in half lengthwise

Canola oil

Sea salt

FOR THE HARISSA YOGURT

¼ cup (50 g) Homemade Thick Yogurt (page 189), or Greek yogurt

1 tbsp (15 ml) fresh lemon juice

1 tbsp (11 g) Harissa (page 186)

Sea salt

TO PLATE

4 medjool dates, cut into slivers

A handful of small fresh mint leaves, for garnish

A handful of small fresh dill leaves, for garnish

Extra virgin olive oil, for garnish

FOR THE FREEKEH

In a colander, drain the freekeh and shake to dry. In a medium saucepan, heat the olive oil. Add the freekeh and cook over moderately high heat, stirring continuously for 1 minute. Add the vegetable stock, season with salt and bring to a boil. Simmer over moderate heat until the liquid reduces enough to see the freekeh, about 8-10 minutes. Reduce the heat to low, cover the pan and continue to cook until the liquid is absorbed and the freekeh is cooked through, about 8-10 minutes. Keep covered and remove from the heat to let the grains rest and continue to steam, about 15 minutes. Fluff the grains with a fork and reserve warm.

FOR THE CARROTS

Meanwhile, preheat the oven to 400°F (205°C). In a large mixing bowl, toss the carrots with a drizzle of canola oil and season with salt. Spread out the carrots in one layer on a parchment-lined baking sheet. Roast for 18-25 minutes, until they start to brown and are semi-soft when pricked with a fork.

FOR THE HARISSA YOGURT

In a small mixing bowl, combine all of the ingredients, season with salt and whisk until combined.

TO PLATE

Spoon the freekeh onto a large serving platter or bowl; arrange the carrots around in a circle, then top with the dates. Drizzle the harissa yogurt around the platter and garnish with the mint, dill and a drizzle of olive oil.

Fresh Beans & Peas with Lemon/Thyme Yogurt and Sumac

The trick with shelling beans is that they need to be blanched in salty water. How salty? Salty like the sea ... and if you don't know how salty the sea is, drop this book immediately and book a ticket to the nearest ocean. Otherwise, let's continue with the recipe. Look at this recipe as a template. You can dress it up or down as desired, substituting different types of beans and peas as you like. The more colors and textures that you have, the better it will end up.

6–8 SERVINGS

FOR THE LEMON/THYME YOGURT

½ cup (100 g) Homemade Thick Yogurt (page 189), or Greek yogurt

1 lemon, finely zested and juiced

2 garlic cloves, finely grated

3 tbsp (6 g) fresh thyme leaves, plus extra for garnish

Pinch of cayenne

Sea salt

FOR THE BEANS & PEAS

Sea salt

3 lb (1.36 kg) fresh shelling beans & peas (cranberry, edamame, young fava and English peas), shelled

2 lb (908 g) assorted pole beans (Romano, yellow and purple wax and Dragon Tongue)

TO FINISH

Sea salt

12 young pea shoots

3 tbsp (45 ml) extra virgin olive oil, plus more for garnish

1 tsp (3 g) ground sumac, plus extra for garnish

FOR THE LEMON/THYME YOGURT

In a small bowl, combine all of the ingredients, season with salt and whisk until combined.

FOR THE BEANS & PEAS

Fill a large bowl halfway with ice. In a medium saucepan of salted boiling water, cook the shelling beans and peas until they start to soften, about 2-3 minutes. Pour the cooking liquid, beans and peas into the ice bowl to cool completely. Drain and pat dry with a paper towel.

Fill a large bowl with salted ice water. In a large saucepan of salted boiling water, cook the pole beans until they are tender but still crisp, about 2 minutes. Drain immediately and immerse in the ice water to cool completely. Drain and pat dry with a paper towel.

TO FINISH

In a large bowl, toss the shelling beans, peas and pole beans with the olive oil and sumac and season with salt. Spoon the mixture into a serving bowl and drizzle with the lemon/thyme yogurt, a sprinkling of sumac, a few leaves of thyme and the pea shoots.

CHEF'S TIP: If you cannot find young fava beans, you can substitute mature fava beans, but you must peel them a second time. This is done after they are cooked and cooled.

Jeweled Rice

The Persians turned rice cookery into an art form. To me, this dish conjures up visions of Persian opulence. So why not eat like Persian royalty? The basmati rice gets flavored with saffron, cardamom and cinnamon. The "jewels"—a garnish of nuts, dried fruit and rose petals—make for a presentation that is truly magnificent and guaranteed to turn some heads. Serve with almost any meat, poultry or fish recipe from the Large Plates chapter.

6 SERVINGS

FOR THE RICE

2 tbsp (28 g) unsalted butter

½ cinnamon stick

6 cardamom pods, crushed lightly

3 cups (590 g) basmati rice, rinsed and dried

Sea salt

3 cups (710 ml) water

¼ cup (60 ml) Saffron Water "Tea" (page 199)

FOR THE "JEWELS"

¼ cup (37 g) golden raisins

¼ cup (33 g) dried apricots, sliced

¼ cup (36 g) dried barberries or currants, soaked in hot water for 2 minutes

¼ cup (36 g) blanched whole almonds, fried in oil (see page 205)

¼ cup (31 g) Iranian pistachios, lightly crushed

Edible rose pedals or dried rosebuds, for garnish

Micro cilantro or small cilantro leaves, for garnish

Chives cut into 1" (3 cm) pieces, for garnish

FOR THE RICE

In a medium saucepan, melt the butter. Add the cinnamon stick and cardamom pods and cook over moderate- high heat until the butter starts to brown lightly, about 1 minute. Add the rinsed basmati rice and stir to coat with the butter; season with salt. Add the water and bring to a boil. Continue to cook until most of the water is absorbed. Add the saffron water and swirl with a spoon, making sure not to completely mix the rice and saffron water. Cover and cook over very low heat until the water is completely absorbed, about 15 minutes. Remove from the heat and let the rice stand, covered, for 5–7 minutes. Fluff the rice with a fork and keep warm.

FOR THE "JEWELS"

Spoon the rice into a large serving platter and garnish with the "jewels."

CHEF'S TIP: When cooking long-grain rice such as basmati, you want to make sure that it's washed well. By washing it, you are loosening the starch to keep it fluffy and light and not sticky, as each grain of rice has to "stand" on its own. To do so, place the rice in a fine-mesh colander or strainer and rinse under cold water while gently swishing it around with your fingertips until the water runs clear.

Lobster Orzo Salad

Orzo is rice-shaped pasta that is very popular in Greek cuisine. Here it's tossed in a lobster stock reduction laced with yogurt, poached lobster and roasted tomatoes. Naturally, this recipe works well as an accompaniment to many fish dishes, but I urge you to try it with meat dishes such as Grilled Lamb Chops (page 102) for an unusual surf and turf.

4–6 SERVINGS

FOR THE POACHED LOBSTER

2 tbsp (30 ml) champagne vinegar

¼ cup (45 g) kosher salt

1 (1½ lb [680 g]) live lobster

FOR THE ORZO SALAD

2 cups (480 ml) Lobster Stock (page 192)

1 cup (200 g) orzo

3 tbsp (39 g) Homemade Thick Yogurt (page 189), or Greek yogurt

6 Roasted Garlic Cloves (page 68)

1 tbsp (2 g) tarragon leaves, chopped, plus leaves for garnish

1 green onion, thinly sliced

Sea salt

1 cup (165 g) Roasted Tomatoes (page 204)

FOR THE POACHED LOBSTER

Fill a small stockpot with water, add the vinegar and salt and bring to a boil over moderate-high heat. Lay the lobster on a cutting board. Place one hand on the tail and hold it flat against the board. With the other hand, place the tip of a large sharp knife about 1 inch (3 cm) behind the eyes, where the body meets the tail, with the blade facing the head. In one quick motion, plunge the tip of the knife straight down through the head and bring the blade down to the board to kill the lobster instantly. Reduce the heat under the boiling water to maintain a simmer, drop the lobster into the water, cover and cook gently until the shell is bright red, 9–12 minutes.

While the lobster cooks, fill a large bowl with equal amounts of ice and water. Carefully remove the lobster from the pot and plunge into the ice water and cool completely; drain. Twist the tail off of the lobster body; crack the claws and knuckles and remove the meat. Using scissors, cut along the underside of the tail shell and remove the meat. Remove and discard the dark intestinal veins; cut the tails into 2 inch (5 cm) pieces and reserve in a large mixing bowl along with the claws and knuckles. Reserve the head and shell for making stock.

FOR THE ORZO SALAD

Place the lobster stock in a saucepan and bring it to a simmer over moderate-high heat. Reduce the stock to about ½ cup (120 ml). Place in a large bowl and refrigerate.

Meanwhile, in a medium saucepan of boiling salted water, cook the orzo until al dente, about 9 minutes. Drain and rinse well under cold water, and shake dry. Combine the yogurt, roasted garlic, tarragon and green onions with the reduced lobster stock and whisk. Combine with the reserved lobster and orzo, then season with salt. Garnish with the tarragon leaves and roasted tomatoes.

Parsnip Lentils with Hazelnuts

Lentils are a staple in the Mediterranean diet, but I've never seen them served this way. The pureed parsnips add a nutty, almost sweet creaminess to the earthy lentils. Look for smaller parsnips, as the larger ones tend to be woody.

6 SERVINGS

FOR THE LENTILS

1 cup (192 g) lentils, rinsed

½ small onion, halved

1 celery stalk

2 fresh thyme sprigs

1 fresh bay leaf

1 cup (240 ml) vegetable stock

2 cups (480 ml) water

Sea salt

FOR THE PARSNIPS

2 tbsp (30 ml) canola oil

2 medium parsnips (about 8 oz [228 g]), peeled, cored and cut diagonally into 3" (8 cm) strips

Sea salt

1 medium parsnip (about 4 oz [114 g]), peeled and cut into thin coins

2 tbsp (30 ml) whole milk

1½ cups (360 ml) water

¼ lb (114 g) unsalted butter, diced, cold

TO FINISH

3 tbsp (45 ml) Brown Butter (page 203)

2 tbsp (30 ml) fresh lemon juice

½ cup (68 g) hazelnuts, toasted and chopped (see page 205)

2 tbsp (6 g) chives, finely chopped

¼ cup (15 g) mint, roughly chopped

FOR THE LENTILS

In a medium saucepan, combine the lentils with the onion, celery, thyme, bay leaf, vegetable stock and water. Season with salt and bring to a boil. Simmer over moderate heat until tender but not falling apart, 15–20 minutes. Drain well and let cool in a large bowl. Remove and discard the onion, celery, thyme and bay leaf.

FOR THE PARSNIPS

In a large frying pan, over moderate heat, add the canola oil and the parsnip strips; season with salt. Cook for 15–20 minutes, stirring frequently, until the parsnips start to caramelize and are tender but not mushy.

Meanwhile, in a medium saucepan, cover the parsnip coins with the milk and water, add a pinch of salt and bring to a boil. Simmer over moderately low heat until the parsnips are tender, about 10–13 minutes. Drain, reserving 3 tablespoons (45 ml) of the cooking liquid. Transfer the parsnips and the reserved liquid to a blender and puree on high. With the motor running, slowly add the butter, then season with salt.

TO FINISH

Combine the cooked lentils with the caramelized parsnips; add the parsnip puree and warm through over moderate heat, stirring occasionally. Add the brown butter and lemon juice. Spoon the lentils into a bowl and garnish with the hazelnuts, chives and mint.

Broccolini with Grilled Lemon, Pine Nuts and Aleppo Chile

I love broccolini. The entire vegetable is edible, but my favorite part is the stalk. To me, the flavor is less bitter than broccoli and with a sweetness that is closer to asparagus without the astringency. These flavors are balanced with some heat from the Aleppo chile and a good amount of acid from the grilled lemons. It may seem that grilling lemons is too much work, but, trust me, it's not. To make starting the grill worthwhile, pair this with the Charcoal Grilled Chicken Skewers (page 96) or a simple grilled piece of chicken or steak.

6–8 SERVINGS

Sea salt

1 lb (454 g) broccolini

3 lemons, seeded, 1 thinly sliced crosswise, 2 halved

Canola oil, for brushing

1 small shallot, finely minced

1 tbsp (15 ml) fresh lemon juice

1 tbsp (14 g) unsalted butter

4 tbsp (60 ml) extra virgin olive oil

¼ cup (17 g) pine nuts

1 tbsp (4 g) flat-leaf parsley, finely chopped

1 tbsp (3 g) finely minced chives

Ground Aleppo chile, to garnish

Preheat a gas or charcoal grill to high heat.

Fill a large bowl with salted ice water. In a large saucepan of salted boiling water, cook the broccolini until almost tender, about 3 minutes. Drain immediately and immerse in the ice water to cool completely. Drain and pat dry with a paper towel.

Brush the lemon slices and halves with oil and grill over high heat. Turn the slices and cook until lightly charred, 2-3 minutes total. Grill the halves on the cut side until heavily charred, around 5-7 minutes, and let cool. Transfer the slices to a cutting board and let cool. Finely dice and reserve in a mixing bowl. Squeeze the grilled halves to extract the juice. Strain the juice and combine with the diced grilled lemon. Add the shallot, fresh lemon juice and season with salt. Let marinate for 10 minutes.

Meanwhile, in a large skillet over moderate heat, add the butter and 1 tablespoon (15 ml) of the olive oil. Once the butter starts to bubble, add the pine nuts and stir continually until golden, about 2 minutes. Remove the pine nuts from the pan with a slotted spoon. Add the broccolini and toss to warm up for about 5 minutes, adding a small amount of olive oil if necessary.

Combine the rest of the olive oil with the grilled lemon and shallot mixture; add the parsley and chives and whisk to combine.

Divide the broccolini among individual serving plates. Spoon some of the grilled lemon mixture over it, and garnish with the pine nuts and a sprinkling of Aleppo chile.

CHEF'S TIP: Alternatively, you could grill the broccolini after blanching for a smoky charred flavor.

Roasted Baby Eggplant with Tahini, Pine Nuts and Pomegranate

You can't talk about Mediterranean cuisine without talking about eggplants. They are found on tables for breakfast, lunch and dinner. Eggplant comes in a wide variety of different shapes, colors and sizes. Here, baby or "Indian" eggplant get scored and roasted in a hot pan with olive oil, thyme and garlic. The accompaniments of tahini sauce, toasted pine nuts, mint and pomegranate pay homage to the classic flavors of baba ganoush.

6 SERVINGS

FOR THE EGGPLANTS

12 baby eggplants, washed

Sea salt

2 sprigs of fresh thyme

2 garlic cloves, finely grated

½ cup (120 ml) olive oil

TO PLATE

¼ cup (54 g) Tahini Sauce (page 175)

2 tbsp (26 g) Homemade Thick Yogurt (page 189), thinned out with a splash of lemon juice and yogurt whey or water

3 tbsp (45 ml) pomegranate molasses

Seeds of ½ medium pomegranate

3 tbsp (24 g) pine nuts, toasted (see page 205)

4 tbsp (6.4 g) fresh mint, torn

Maldon salt

Extra virgin olive oil, for garnish

FOR THE EGGPLANTS

Cut the eggplant in half lengthwise. With the tip of a sharp paring knife, score the flesh lightly in a diamond cross-hatch pattern by making 3 long cuts, cutting at a steep angle, and then rotating the eggplant to make another set of similar cuts. Sprinkle salt over the cut surface. Set aside, cut-side up, for 30–60 minutes. Preheat the oven to 400°F (205°C).

Gently squeeze the eggplant to extract the liquid and wipe them dry with a paper towel. In a large mixing bowl, toss the eggplant with the thyme, garlic and olive oil. Arrange each half, cut-side down, on a parchment-lined baking sheet and roast for 20–30 minutes. The eggplant will collapse and the bottoms will be a deep caramel color.

TO PLATE

Place the roasted eggplants onto a platter so the cut side is up. Drizzle the tahini sauce in thin streams over the eggplants. Repeat with the yogurt and pomegranate molasses. Finish with the pomegranate seeds, pine nuts, mint leaves, a light sprinkling of Maldon salt and a drizzle of olive oil.

CHEF'S TIP: Salt first! Some people complain that eggplant is bitter. This little trick helps draw out moisture from the eggplant, which makes it less bitter. I also feel that it makes the eggplant soak up less oil. It's simple. After splitting the eggplant, salt the cut flesh and let it sit for 30–60 minutes, drain, pat dry and proceed with cooking.

Roasted Carrots with Oil-Cured Black Olives and Cumin Yogurt

Choose really young carrots with the tops still attached when they are available, as the results are outstanding. The carrots get roasted in the oven with thyme, which perfumes the carrots while they roast. I'm a huge fan of oil-cured olives, which is the most ancient way of preserving olives. However, the name is misleading because they are typically cured in salt, which draws out the moisture and cures the olives in the process. They lend an earthy, almost salty, caramel-like quality to any dish.

4–6 SERVINGS

FOR THE CARROTS

15 baby carrots, tops trimmed and the carrots scrubbed with a brush under water

3 sprigs of fresh thyme, plus extra picked leaves for garnish

Canola oil

Sea salt

FOR THE CUMIN YOGURT

¼ cup (50 g) Homemade Thick Yogurt (page 189), or Greek yogurt

1 tbsp (15 ml) fresh lemon juice

1 tbsp (4 g) cilantro, finely chopped

2 tsp (4 g) cumin seeds, toasted and ground

Pinch of Urfa pepper

Sea salt

TO PLATE

¼ cup (43 g) oil-cured black olives, pitted and halved

Maldon salt

Extra virgin olive oil, for garnish

FOR THE CARROTS

Preheat the oven to 450°F (232°C). In a large bowl, toss the carrots with the thyme sprigs and a drizzle of canola oil. Season with sea salt and spread out the carrots in one layer on a parchment-lined baking sheet. Roast for 25–30 minutes. The carrots are done when they start to brown and are semi-soft when pricked with a fork. Remove and discard the thyme sprigs.

FOR THE CUMIN YOGURT

In a small bowl, combine all of the ingredients, season with salt and whisk to combine.

TO PLATE

Place the carrots on a platter. Drizzle the cumin yogurt in thin streams over the carrots. Finish with the reserved thyme leaves, oil-cured black olives, a light sprinkling of crunchy salt and a drizzle of olive oil.

Smoky Corn Farina with Tomato Salad

Farina, or cream of wheat, is a fairly bland cereal grain; think of it as grits or polenta. In this recipe the farina is cooked in a savory combination of smoky corn stock and smoked cheese with sweet corn, topped with a refreshing tomato salad. Serve it alongside braised or roasted meats.

4–6 SERVINGS

FOR THE TOMATO SALAD

1 lb (454 g) assorted sizes and colors heirloom tomatoes, cut into wedges

2 tbsp (30 ml) extra virgin olive oil

1 tbsp (15 ml) champagne vinegar

1 small shallot, thinly sliced

Sea salt

Freshly ground black pepper

A handful small basil leaves, for garnish

FOR THE CORN FARINA

1 cup (240 ml) Smoky Corn Stock (page 178) or vegetable stock

1 cup (240 ml) whole milk

5 tbsp (55 g) farina

2 tbsp (28 g) unsalted butter, diced

2 cups (308 g) sweet corn kernels, reserved from making the stock

½ cup (57 g) grated smoked cheddar cheese

Sea salt

FOR THE TOMATO SALAD

In a medium bowl, gently toss the tomatoes with the rest of the ingredients, excluding the basil, and season with salt and pepper.

FOR THE CORN FARINA

Combine the stock and milk in a heavy-bottomed saucepan. Bring to a boil over moderate-high heat, stirring from time to time, being careful not to scorch the milk. Lower the heat to moderate and slowly mix in the farina and stir constantly. Continue to cook for 5–10 minutes, until the farina thickens and large bubbles appear on the surface. Remove from the heat and incorporate the butter, corn kernels and cheese and season with salt. Spoon the farina into a serving bowl, top with the tomato salad and garnish with a few leaves of basil and some freshly ground black pepper.

Spring "Farrotto"

Farro is an ancient grain that has become very popular in recent years. This recipe is very versatile; it works well with seasonal vegetables and garnishes. Don't let the name deter you from making it in the winter with root vegetables. That being said, the spring iteration is by far my favorite. The name is a nod to the way that the farro is cooked, in the style of risotto. Small amounts of liquid are absorbed while stirring until it gets creamy.

8 SERVINGS

FOR THE VEGETABLES

A pinch of baking soda

½ lb (227 g) green asparagus, trimmed and sliced on diagonal into 2" (5 cm) pieces

¼ cup (37 g) English peas, shelled

¼ cup (30 g) fava beans, shelled

16 fiddlehead ferns, trimmed

Canola oil

16 morel mushrooms, halved

Sea salt

16 ramps, trimmed

8 Poached Baby Artichokes (page 72), halved

FOR THE "FARROTTO"

¼ lb (113 g) unsalted butter

1 small onion, finely chopped

Sea salt

2 garlic cloves, sliced

1½ cups (150 g) farro, rinsed and drained

¼ cup (60 ml) dry white wine

6 cups (1.4 L) vegetable stock or water

2 tbsp (20 g) finely grated Pecorino Romano cheese

A large handful of assorted greens (wild arugula, upland cress and young pea shoots), for garnish

Assorted radishes (watermelon, icicle and breakfast), thinly sliced and cut into sticks, for garnish

Chives and chive flowers, for garnish

FOR THE VEGETABLES

Fill a large bowl with salted ice water. Add the baking soda to a large saucepan of salted boiling water; cook the asparagus until it is tender but still crisp, about 2-3 minutes. Remove from the boiling water and immerse in the ice water to cool completely. Drain and pat dry with a paper towel. Repeat with the peas, fava beans and fiddleheads, adjusting cooking times as necessary, depending on the size and the maturity of the vegetables. I suggest that you test it by cooking a small amount first.

Heat a small amount of canola oil in a medium skillet; add the mushrooms, season with salt and cook over moderate heat until fully cooked, about 5-8 minutes.

Divide the ramps into whites and greens. Thinly slice the white part and reserve. Blanch the green tops in the boiling water until bright green, about 45 seconds. Remove from the boiling water and immerse in the ice water to cool completely. Drain and transfer to a blender. Puree on high speed, adding 1 tablespoon (15 ml) water if necessary, scraping the sides of the bowl as needed, until very smooth and bright green, about 5-6 minutes.

FOR THE "FARROTTO"

In a large saucepan, melt half the butter. Add the onion, season with salt and cook over moderate heat until softened, about 3 minutes. Add the garlic and reserved white ramps and cook, stirring, until fragrant, about 1 minute. Add the farro and stir for 1 minute. Turn up the heat to high, add the white wine and simmer until the wine has evaporated, about 2-4 minutes. Lower the heat to moderate. Season with salt and add 1 cup (240 ml) of the stock or water and cook, stirring often, until absorbed. Repeat with the remaining liquid, adding 1 cup (240 ml) at a time and stirring constantly until the farro is tender and creamy, about 30 minutes total.

Stir the vegetables into the farrotto and bring to a boil over moderate heat to warm the vegetables. Remove from the heat, and stir in the ramp puree, remaining butter and pecorino. Adjust the seasoning with salt.

Spoon the farrotto into individual bowls or a platter, top with the morel mushrooms and garnish with a handful of green leaves, a few slices of radishes and chives and flowers.

CHEF'S TIP: If you can find green farro, use it here. The flavor is amazing and the texture is far superior.

Sweet Corn with Feta Fondue and Aleppo Chile

This dish is inspired by Mexican *elote,* which is a popular street food of corn on the cob, brushed with mayonnaise, chile powder and lime. Here the whole ears of corn get charred on the grill then brushed with feta fondue in lieu of the mayo, and Aleppo chiles and smoked hot paprika instead of chile powder.

6 SERVINGS

6 ears fresh sweet corn, husks on

Feta Fondue (page 34)

Ground Aleppo chile, for garnish

Spanish smoked hot paprika, for garnish

1 lime, zested

Sea salt

Preheat a gas or charcoal grill to high heat.

Meanwhile, peel back the cornhusks, keeping them attached. Discard the silk. Fold the husks back over the corn and tie the tops with kitchen string. Place the corn in a large pot or bowl, cover with water and let soak for 20-30 minutes. Remove the corn from the water and shake to remove excess water. Grill the corn in the husks over high heat, turning it often, until the kernels start to blister, about 15-20 minutes. Remove from the grill and let cool slightly. Carefully pull back the husks and transfer the corn to a platter. Brush the feta fondue all over the corn; garnish with a sprinkling of Aleppo chile, paprika, lime zest and a sprinkling of salt.

CHEF'S TIP: Is corn on the cob too messy for your taste? Fine. After grilling the corn, remove the kernels from the cob, then garnish with the feta fondue, spices and lime zest.

Sweet Potatoes with Tamarind and Tahini

Tamarind is referred to as "Indian dates" in the Middle East. It has a unique flavor that is sweet and sour. Here it plays an important roll of adding sweetness and acidity to balance the roasted sweet potatoes and tahini sauce. This recipe would also make a tasty mezze.

4–6 SERVINGS

2 large sweet potatoes, peeled and cut into ½" (13 mm) rounds

Canola oil

Sea salt

¼ cup (54 g) Tahini Sauce (page 175)

3 tbsp (45 ml) tamarind syrup or pomegranate molasses

2 tbsp (8 g) cilantro, coarsely chopped

Maldon salt

Extra virgin olive oil, for garnish

Preheat the oven to 450°F (232°C). In a large bowl, toss the sweet potatoes with a drizzle of canola oil and season with sea salt. Spread out the sweet potatoes in one layer on a parchment-lined baking sheet, and roast for 20–30 minutes, until brown and soft when pricked with a fork.

Place the roasted sweet potatoes on a platter. Drizzle the tahini sauce in thin streams over the sweet potatoes and repeat with the tamarind syrup. Finish with the cilantro, a light sprinkling of Maldon salt and a drizzle of olive oil.

Roasted Butternut Squash with Black Figs, Brown Butter and Blue Cheese

Blue cheese has become one of my favorite cheeses to add balance to sweet dishes. The pairing of figs and blue cheese is a classic one for a reason. The sweetness of the figs balances the funk of the blue cheese, which made me think about which other sweet vegetables or fruits would benefit from a little blue cheese. Butternut squash is on top of the list along with sweet potatoes and beets.

6 SERVINGS

FOR THE ROASTED BUTTERNUT SQUASH

1 large butternut squash, peeled and cut into 1" x 2½" (2.5 x 6.4 cm) wedges

3 tbsp (45 ml) canola oil

2 tsp (16.8 g) Garam Masala (page 181)

1 tbsp (14 g) brown sugar

3 tbsp (42 g) unsalted butter, diced

Sea salt

FOR THE BROWN BUTTER/SHERRY VINEGAR DRESSING

½ lb (226 g) unsalted butter

¼ cup (60 ml) good-quality sherry vinegar

2 tsp (10 g) brown sugar

1 tsp (0.7 g) rosemary leaves, coarsely chopped

1 tbsp (4.8 g) thyme leaves, coarsely chopped, plus more for garnishing

2 tbsp (30 ml) extra virgin olive oil

Sea salt

Fresh ground black pepper

TO PLATE

6 dried black figs, quartered

1 oz (29 g) mild blue cheese, crumbled

2 green onions, thinly sliced

Urfa pepper, for garnish

FOR THE ROASTED BUTTERNUT SQUASH

Preheat the oven to 450°F (232°C). In a large bowl, toss the butternut squash with the canola oil, garam masala, brown sugar and butter. Season with salt and spread out the squash in one layer on a parchment-lined baking sheet. Roast for 30–40 minutes, until the squash gets a deep brown color and is soft when pricked with a fork.

FOR THE BROWN BUTTER/SHERRY VINEGAR DRESSING

In a medium saucepan, melt the butter over moderate heat, whisking occasionally, until the milk solids begin to brown and release a nutty aroma, about 8 minutes. Remove from the heat and while slightly warm, but not hot, add the sherry vinegar and brown sugar, gently whisk, being careful, as it might splatter. Let cool completely, add the herbs and adjust the seasoning with salt and pepper.

TO PLATE

Place the roasted butternut squash on a platter. Drizzle the dressing over the squash. Finish with the figs, blue cheese, green onions, Urfa pepper and reserved thyme.

Young Fava Beans with Green Charmoula

Young fava beans are absolutely delicious and have no resemblance to their starchy, mature and dry relatives. This quick recipe will pair well with many meat-based entrées as a side, or served as part of a mezze selection.

4 SERVINGS

Sea salt

3 lb (1.36 kg) fresh young fava bean pods, shelled (about 2½ cups [375 g])

1½ tbsp (23 ml) extra virgin olive oil

3–5 tbsp (81–135 g) Green Charmoula (page 185)

¼ Preserved Lemon rind (page 196), thinly sliced

¼ cup (60 g) Yogurt Cheese (page 191) or fresh goat cheese

Fill a large bowl halfway with ice. In a medium saucepan of salted boiling water, cook the fava beans until the skins start to loosen, about 2-3 minutes. Pour the cooking liquid and the beans into the ice bowl to cool. Once completely cooled, drain and discard the liquid. To peel, squeeze the fava beans from their skins. In a medium skillet over moderate heat, warm the olive oil and toss the beans to warm, about 1 minute. Add the charmoula and remove from the heat. Season with salt, spoon the warmed beans into a bowl and garnish with the preserved lemon slices and the yogurt cheese.

CHEF'S TIP: You can substitute green chickpeas or soybeans for similar results.

Dessert

When I was growing up, most meals ended with fresh and dried fruit, nuts and tea. Occasionally, a thin sliver of a light cake was served after dinner. Desserts and pastries were rarely eaten in the way that they are in the West. Classic Middle Eastern desserts such as baklava and kunafa were typically served in the afternoon along with coffee and tea or at celebrations and special occasions.

Many of the dishes in this chapter were inspired by the flavors of classic Mediterranean sweets. To me, these recipes embody the essence of the cuisine without being traditional.

Arabic Coffee Cream

This rich yet light cream is a perfect ending to a heavy meal when you are looking for something with more substance. The addition of the cardamom and cloves adds a fragrant cooling effect to the coffee cream. I like serving it along with Ancient Arabic Coffee (page 166) with a few medjool dates and dried figs.

4–6 SERVINGS, DEPENDING ON SIZE OF RAMEKIN

½ cup plus 2 tbsp (150 ml) whole milk

2 cardamom pods, lightly crushed

3 whole cloves

½ tsp saffron threads, crushed with fingertips

½ cup (40 g) coarsely ground, light roasted coffee beans, or 1½ tbsp (4.5 g) instant espresso

4 egg yolks

¼ cup (50 g) sugar

½ cup (120 ml) heavy cream

Preheat the oven to 400°F (205°C). In a medium saucepan, combine the milk, cardamom, cloves and saffron. Simmer over moderate heat for 5 minutes. Remove from the heat; add the coffee or instant espresso, stir and cover to infuse for 1 hour. Strain the milk, pushing on the coffee to extract as much flavor as possible; discard the coffee and spices. Reheat the infused milk gently.

Set 4–6 small ovenproof cups or ramekins in a baking pan. In a medium bowl, whisk the egg yolks with the sugar until pale. Slowly whisk in the hot milk, then add the heavy cream. Strain through a fine-mesh strainer into a plastic pitcher, refrigerate for 30 minutes, then skim the foam off the top and discard. Pour the custard into the ramekins. Add enough hot water to the baking dish to reach halfway up the sides of the ramekins. Cover with foil and bake for 30–40 minutes, until they are almost set but still slightly jiggly in the center. Transfer the ramekins to a rack and let cool to room temperature. Cover and refrigerate for at least 3 hours before serving.

Arak-Poached Pears with Sweet Cheese

The inescapable poached pear gets a Mediterranean makeover. Arak is the perfect accent for the pears and the sweet cheese. The anisey flavor of arak makes it a perfect match for most fruit, so it is a natural pairing. This recipe goes well with the Roasted Lemonade with Mint and Arak (page 170) for a full arak experience.

6 SERVINGS

FOR THE ARAK-POACHED PEARS
3 cups (720 ml) water
1½ cups (300 g) sugar
3 cardamom pods, lightly crushed
3 Bartlett pears
1 tbsp (15 ml) fresh lemon juice
½ cup (120 ml) arak or high-quality ouzo
Sea salt

TO SERVE
½ cup (114 g) mascarpone cheese
½ cup (123 g) fresh ricotta

FOR THE ARAK-POACHED PEARS
Combine the water, sugar and cardamom in a medium saucepan and bring to a simmer over moderate-high heat.

Meanwhile, peel and cut the pears in half and remove the cores of the pears with a melon baller. Place the pear halves in the simmering liquid, making sure that they are fully submerged. Add more water if needed. Add the lemon juice, arak and a pinch of salt, cover with a parchment paper circle, reduce the heat to low and continue to cook gently, turning them occasionally, for 15–20 minutes, until the pears are cooked through and are soft when pierced with the tip of a knife.

TO SERVE
Transfer the pears to a serving bowl. Increase the heat and reduce the liquid to a thick syrup, similar to honey in texture. Drizzle half the syrup over the pears and leave to cool.

Meanwhile, in a mixing bowl, whisk together the remaining poaching syrup with the mascarpone and ricotta and refrigerate until well chilled. Top the pears with the sweet cheese and serve at room temperature or slightly chilled.

CHEF'S TIP: You can substitute any seasonal fruit. I especially like stone fruit in the summer. Adjust the cooking time and liquid proportions according to how ripe the fruit is.

Chocolate & Ras el Hanout Ice Cream with Olive Oil and Sea Salt

I love combining chocolate with spicy elements. Ras el hanout works really well here because it has a complex flavor profile that stands up to chocolate. Olive oil and chocolate may seem like an odd combination, but it's magnificent. The first time I encountered olive oil and sea salt mixed with chocolate was in Spain. It blew me away, and I've loved that combination ever since. Serve this with the Olive Oil Cake (page 158) and some orange segments for a more composed dessert.

8 SERVINGS

4 oz (113 g) best-quality dark chocolate, finely chopped

3 oz (85 g) best-quality milk chocolate, finely chopped

1 cup (240 ml) whole milk

1½ cups (360 ml) heavy cream

1 tbsp (5 g) unsweetened cocoa powder

2 tsp (4.5 g) Ras El Hanout (page 182)

6 egg yolks

½ cup (100 g) sugar

Maldon salt

Fruity extra virgin olive oil

Place both chocolates in a medium heatproof bowl. Set the bowl over a saucepan of barely simmering water. Stir the chocolate until melted and smooth. Set the melted chocolate aside; let cool slightly. Whisk the milk, heavy cream, cocoa powder and ras el hanout in a medium saucepan over moderate heat until the mixture begins to boil; remove from the heat and set aside.

Whisk the egg yolks and sugar in a medium bowl until very thick ribbons form, about 2 minutes. Whisking constantly, slowly add hot milk and cream mixture to the egg yolk mixture. Return to the saucepan. Add the melted chocolate and whisk to blend. Stir over low heat until slightly thickened, about 5 minutes. Strain the liquid through a fine-mesh strainer and place in a medium bowl; place over a large bowl of ice water. Transfer to a storage container and refrigerate for at least 2 hours, but preferably overnight. Pour the ice cream base into an ice cream maker and churn it according to the manufacturer's instructions. Freeze until the ice cream is firm.

Scoop the ice cream and serve with a sprinkling of crunchy salt and a drizzle of olive oil.

> **CHEF'S TIP:** This recipe will also work with any sweet spices. I like yellow curry mix as a substitute for the ras el hanout.

Fried Milk Pudding (Leche Frita)

This is one of the most unique dessert recipes that I've encountered. This classic Spanish dessert is a perfect balance of a firm, sweet, cold, milk-pudding center encased in a warm and crunchy fried outer shell. In this variation, I omitted the cinnamon sugar dusting and added saffron and fresh vanilla bean to the mix for a more floral and luxurious pudding. You can experiment with different combinations of spices. Another combination that I like is coriander and cardamom.

8–10 SERVINGS

FOR THE MILK PUDDING

4 cups (960 ml) whole milk

1 tsp (0.9 g) saffron threads, crushed with fingertips

½ fresh vanilla bean, seeds scraped

½ cinnamon stick

Peel of 1 lemon

¾ cup (150 g) sugar

½ cup (64 g) cornstarch

About ½ cup (120 ml) water

TO FINISH

½ cup (57 g) all-purpose flour, for dusting

2 eggs, beaten with 1 tsp (5 ml) milk

1½ cups (96 g) panko breadcrumbs, finely buzzed in a food processor

Canola oil, for frying

FOR THE MILK PUDDING

In a medium saucepan, simmer the milk, saffron, vanilla bean and seeds, cinnamon stick and lemon peel, over moderate heat, about 5–7 minutes. Add the sugar and whisk until dissolved. Remove from the heat and let stand for 20–30 minutes to infuse. Lightly oil a 12 inch (30 cm) glass baking pan and line with plastic film, leaving 2 inches (5 cm) of plastic film overhang on the sides.

Strain the infused milk and discard the vanilla bean, cinnamon stick and lemon peel. Return the milk to the heat. Whisk together the cornstarch and water in a small bowl and gradually pour the cornstarch mixture into the infused milk, whisking constantly until combined. Cook over moderate heat, stirring constantly with a wooden spoon, until thick, about 5 minutes. It should be thick and smooth. If it appears slightly lumpy, whisk to remove the lumps, being careful not to scrape the pan. Immediately transfer to the lined pan and cover with plastic wrap so it touches the surface of the pudding. Cool to room temperature, then refrigerate for a minimum of 3 hours, up to overnight. Using the plastic film to release the custard from the sidse of the pan, remove and cut into desired shapes. I like 2 inch (5 cm) squares.

TO FINISH

Put the flour, egg wash and breadcrumbs in 3 separate shallow bowls. Dust the custard with flour, tapping off the excess, dip in the egg wash, remove with a fork and let the excess egg wash drip and roll in the breadcrumbs.

In a large, heavy pot no more than half filled with oil, or a deep fryer, heat the oil to 350°F (177°C). Working in batches, carefully lower the pudding into the oil and fry until golden, turning occasionally, about 2–5 minutes. Remove from the oil and drain briefly on absorbent towels. Serve immediately.

Olive Oil Cake with Orange Blossom

My earliest memories of being in a kitchen were always baking cakes with my mother. I would sit on the counter next to her and watch her sift the flour, crack the egg and eyeball every measurement. If we didn't have an ingredient, she would substitute ingredients and somehow the cakes always worked. I've always joked that my mother measured flour by the handful. When she gave me a "recipe" for a cake, I looked at her hand, compared them to my hands, and we both laughed. You are in luck; this recipe has "real" measurements.

10-12 SERVINGS

FOR THE CAKE

Unsalted butter, as needed for greasing the pan

1¾ cups (219 g) all-purpose flour, plus extra for dusting

¼ cup (60 ml) fresh orange juice

2 tbsp (40 g) orange marmalade, finely chopped

1 cup (200 g) sugar

½ cup (100 g) Homemade Thick Yogurt (page 189), or Greek yogurt

3 eggs

1 cup (240 ml) fruity extra virgin olive oil

3 tbsp (19 g) almond flour

1½ tsp (6.9 g) baking powder

¼ tsp baking soda

¼ tsp sea salt

TO SERVE

1 cup (200 g) sugar

½ cup (120 ml) water

1 tsp (5 ml) orange blossom water

1 tbsp (15 ml) fruity extra virgin olive oil

Homemade Thick Yogurt (page 189), flavored with a few drops of orange blossom water and honey, to serve

FOR THE CAKE

Preheat the oven to 350°F (177°C). Butter a 9" x 5" (23 x 13 cm) loaf pan or 9" (23 cm) round cake pan and dust lightly with flour. In a medium bowl, combine the orange juice, marmalade, sugar, yogurt, eggs and olive oil and whisk until the sugar is dissolved.

In another bowl, whisk together the flour, almond flour, baking powder, baking soda and salt. Gently stir the dry ingredients into the wet ones. Pour the batter into the prepared pan. Bake for 50-60 minutes, until it is golden and a wooden skewer inserted into the center comes out clean.

TO SERVE

Meanwhile, in a small saucepan, combine the sugar and water, bring to a boil and remove from the heat to slightly cool down. Add the orange blossom water and whisk in the olive oil. As soon as the cake comes out of the oven, start brushing with the hot syrup using a pastry brush. Allow the syrup to soak in for a minute before repeating again. Once the cake has cooled down a little, remove from the pan and leave to cool completely. Serve with the yogurt flavored with the orange blossom water and honey.

Pistachio & Sour Cherry Baklava Roll

Baklava comes in many different shapes and sizes and with a variety of fillings. Just like most people who are passionate about food, I have my preferences. I don't want anything to do with the super sweet baklava with walnuts and honey. This version has sour cherries and a saffron/thyme spiced syrup—not traditional, but utterly delicious.

9 SERVINGS

FOR THE SPICED SYRUP

1 cup (200 g) sugar

½ cup (120 ml) water

1 fresh thyme sprig

1 tsp (5 ml) Saffron Water "Tea" (page 199)

Zest and juice of 1 lemon

FOR THE BAKLAVA

2 cups (248 g) pistachios, plus extra, finely crushed, to garnish

1 cup (115 g) dried sour cherries, finely chopped

½ tsp Ras El Hanout (page 182)

½ cup (100 g) sugar

½ lb (227 g) unsalted butter, melted

9 sheets (8 oz [227 g]) phyllo dough, thawed

FOR THE SPICED SYRUP

In a medium saucepan, combine the sugar and water and bring to a boil. Remove from the heat. Add the thyme, saffron water, lemon zest and juice. Cover and let the flavors infuse for 20-30 minutes or until it cools completely. Remove and discard the lemon zest and thyme. The syrup can be refrigerated for up to 2 weeks.

FOR THE BAKLAVA

Preheat the oven to 350°F (177°C).

In a food processor, pulse the pistachios to medium fine, being careful not to form a paste, scraping the sides of the bowl as needed. Combine the pistachios with the sour cherries, ras el hanout, sugar and a little drizzle of the spiced syrup.

Warm the butter in a small saucepan. Unroll the phyllo dough, keeping it under a damp towel to prevent it from drying out. Brush some of the butter on the bottom of a baking sheet. Lay the phyllo with the long side horizontally on a cutting board. Lightly brush one sheet of phyllo with butter; repeat with two more sheets of phyllo. Spread a thin layer of the pistachio mixture, about 3-4 tablespoons (45-60 g), in an even layer over the phyllo, leaving 1 inch (3 cm) of phyllo bare on the left and right sides. Place a long wooden stick or chopstick at one of the short ends of the phyllo. Fold the phyllo over the stick and begin to roll it up loosely to form a thin, long roll.

Gently scrunch the roll, accordion style, with your fingers to make it wrinkly. Gently pull the roll off the stick and place on the buttered sheet pan. Repeat with the remaining dough and filling. Brush a thin layer of butter over the top and cut each roll into 3 equal-size pieces. Bake for 30-45 minutes, until golden and crisp. Remove from the oven, let cool slightly and pour some of the syrup over, making sure to pour slowly and evenly. It will take a minute for the phyllo to absorb the syrup; add more syrup if you prefer sweeter baklava. Leave to cool for 10 minutes, recut the rolls and garnish with crushed pistachios.

CHEF'S TIP: The diameter of the wooden stick or the chopstick will make a huge difference in the final texture of the baklava. A smaller diameter will make a denser roll and a larger diameter will result in a flakier roll. I suggest that you experiment with it to see what works best for you.

Pomegranate & Rose Petal Granita

After a hearty meal, the last thing that I want is to be weighed down by a heavy dessert. This light and refreshing granita is a perfect end to the meal, in my opinion. The beautiful thing about granitas in general is that they stand on their own or they can be combined with other elements to make a composed dessert. The sweetened condensed milk gives more body and richness. Try it alongside the Roasted Peaches with Goat Cheese and Pistachios (page 163); just omit the sweetened condensed milk.

4–6 SERVINGS

½ cup (120 ml) water

1 tbsp (2.9 g) dried rose buds

¼ cup (50 g) sugar

2 cups (480 ml) pomegranate juice

1 tbsp (15 ml) fresh lime juice

2 drops of rose water

Seeds of 1 medium pomegranate

Candied rose petals, optional

Sweetened condensed milk, optional

In a small saucepan, combine the water with the rose buds and bring to a boil. Simmer over moderate heat for 2 minutes. Add the sugar and stir until dissolved. Remove from the heat and let the flavors infuse for up to 2 hours. Add the pomegranate juice, lime juice and rose water and whisk and combine. In a fine-mesh strainer, strain the liquid into a glass casserole and push down the solids to extract all of the essence from the rose petals. Discard the rose petals and freeze for 3–4 hours or overnight. Once the granita is frozen, use a fork to scrape the ice and spoon the granita into chilled glasses or serving bowls. Sprinkle with the pomegranate seeds and garnish with candied rose petals and sweetened condensed milk if you desire.

Roasted Peaches with Goat Cheese and Pistachios

The combination of fruit and cheese, especially goat cheese, is a natural one. Look for a soft goat cheese that isn't too pungent. If you are not able to find one, just cut it with a little cream cheese to mellow out the flavor. Roasting the peaches makes them super luscious and soft. Be careful not to overcook them. They will turn into mush, which, by the way, isn't a bad thing. I've done that in the past and ended up eating the peaches warm with a scoop of vanilla ice cream—divine. When peaches aren't available, I like to poach dried apricots in a syrup flavored with thyme, and stuff them with goat cheese that is sweetened with a little honey.

8 SERVINGS

¼ cup (50 g) sugar

1 tbsp (14 g) brown sugar

4 large, ripe but firm peaches, halved and pitted

Sea salt

2 fresh thyme sprigs, plus picked leaves for garnish

½ cup (137 g) soft goat cheese

2 tbsp (30 ml) honey mixed with 2 tbsp (30 ml) warm water

¼ cup (31 g) pistachios, lightly crushed

Preheat the oven to 400°F (205°C).

Heat a large ovenproof skillet over moderate heat and mix together both sugars in a small bowl.

Sprinkle the cut side of the peaches with three-fourths of the sugar mixture and season with salt. Place the peaches, cut side down, in the skillet and cook for 2-3 minutes, until the peaches start to caramelize. Sprinkle the remaining sugar on top of the peaches, place the thyme sprigs in the middle and cover with foil. Roast the peaches for 7-10 minutes. Remove from the oven and flip the peaches so they are cut side up. Uncover and continue to roast for another 5-8 minutes, until tender, basting occasionally. Remove from the oven and discard the thyme.

Transfer the peaches to a serving platter, spooning any roasting liquid over the top; let cool slightly, about 5 minutes. Garnish with the goat cheese, a drizzle of the honey syrup, pistachios and a few leaves of picked thyme.

Drink

The traditional beverages served in the region vary greatly from country to country. In this chapter, I wanted to showcase recipes beyond mint tea and Turkish coffee. These eastern Mediterranean-inspired beverages pair well with the dishes featured in this book.

Ancient Arabic Coffee

There are two types of coffee served in the Middle East. The first is the thick "Turkish" type, which is prepared with roasted and finely ground coffee beans, ground cardamom and sometimes sugar. It's always served in a small cup, allowing the coffee grounds to settle in the bottom of the cup before drinking. The second is a filtered, lighter and more aromatic version that is thinner in appearance but not in flavor. It is sometimes referred to as Bedouin coffee. My mother prepared ancient Arabic coffee for special occasions. I always loved serving it to our guests. I ran around filling the very small cups halfway full and I continued to refill the guests' cups until they shook their empty glass, an Arabic ritual that signals that they did not want more coffee.

5–10 SERVINGS

3 cups (720 ml) water

6 cardamom pods, lightly crushed

¼ cup (20 g) light roasted coffee beans, coarsely ground

2 whole cloves

2 tbsp (30 ml) Saffron Water "Tea" (page 199)

In a medium saucepan, combine the water and cardamom. Bring to a boil and simmer over moderate heat for 5 minutes. Remove from the heat; add the coffee beans, stir and cover to infuse for 20–25 minutes. Strain the liquid through a very fine-mesh or coffee filter and discard the coffee and cardamom. Add the cloves and saffron water and let steep for 3–5 minutes; serve immediately or reserve warm.

Hibiscus Tea with Dark Spices

Hibiscus has a tart, cranberry-like flavor that is very popular in the Levant and Egypt. The spices and sugar level can be adjusted according to your personal taste and preference. Just remember, you can always add more sugar, but you can't take it out.

ABOUT 2 QUARTS (1.9 L)

8 cups (1.9 L) water

1 cup (22 g) dried hibiscus flowers

6 whole cloves

4 cardamom pods, lightly crushed

½ cinnamon stick

1–1½ cups (200–250 g) sugar

In a medium saucepan, combine the water with the hibiscus and the spices. Bring to a boil and simmer over moderate heat for 10 minutes. Add the sugar and stir until dissolved. Remove from the heat and let the flavors infuse for up to 2 hours. Strain the liquid and discard the spices and hibiscus. Refrigerate until cold and serve over ice.

Roasted Lemonade with Mint and Arak

Arak, distilled from grapes and anise, is an alcoholic beverage popular in the Levant. For a nonalcoholic version, omit the arak and add 1 tablespoon (6 g) of finely ground anise seeds to the lemonade for a similar flavor profile.

8 SERVINGS

6 lemons, ends squared off, halved and seeds picked out

2–3 cups (400–600 g) sugar (depending on how sweet you like it)

3½–4 cups (830–960 ml) water

1 cup (240 ml) fresh lemon juice

¼ teaspoon sea salt

Fresh mint sprigs

Arak, high-quality ouzo or any other anise-flavored liqueur

Preheat the oven to 350°F (177°C).

In a small bowl, toss the lemons with 1 cup (200 g) of the sugar. Place on a roasting pan cut side up, place in the oven and roast until the sugar starts to caramelize and the edges of the lemons start to brown, about 20–30 minutes. Flip the lemons over and finish roasting for another 10–15 minutes. The sugar will caramelize on the bottom of the pan. Deglaze with ½ cup (120 ml) of the water, remove from the oven and cool to room temperature.

Place the cooled lemons and cooking liquid in a food processor and puree for 2–3 minutes, until most of the lemons are broken down. You may need to add another ½ cup (120 ml) water. Strain the roasted lemon puree into a bowl and discard the solids; whisk together the puree with the remaining 2½–3 cups (690–720 ml) water, the lemon juice, salt and the remaining 1–2 cups (200–400 g) sugar to taste.

In a glass, muddle the mint with a small amount of ice. Fill ¾ of the glass with lemonade, then add arak, strain into an ice-filled glass and garnish with a mint sprig.

Sour Cherry & Rose Petal Sharbat

This aromatic and refreshing beverage is prefect on a hot summer day. I remember walking around the markets in Jordan and hearing glasses clicking—the signal of the wandering drink vendors—and suddenly getting thirsty. The sugar level can be adjusted to your liking, adding or subtracting as desired.

4–6 SERVINGS

4 cups (960 ml) water

1 tbsp (2.9 g) dried rose buds

2 cups (310 g) pitted sour cherries, fresh or frozen, a few reserved for garnish

2 cups (400 g) sugar

A splash of rose water

Organic rose petals, for garnish, optional

In a medium saucepan, combine the water with the rose buds and bring to a boil, simmer over moderate heat for 10 minutes, add the sour cherries and continue to simmer for 5 more minutes. Add the sugar and stir until dissolved. Remove from the heat and let the flavors infuse for up to 2 hours. In a fine-mesh strainer, strain the liquid and push down the solids to extract all of the essence from the sour cherries. Discard the cherries and refrigerate the liquid until cold. Serve over ice with a few drops of rose water. Garnish with rose petals and sour cherries if you wish.

Warm Apple Cider with Caraway

At Saffron, we serve this recipe in the fall, when fresh-pressed apple cider is available. Sometimes it is even spiked with rye whiskey or aquavit. I love the scent that is emitted from simmering apple cider with sweet spices. It's comforting and soothing. Caraway has a very unique flavor. The earthy, anisey, almost minty tones make it a perfect match for sweeter preparations.

4 SERVINGS

4 cups (960 ml) apple cider

1 tsp (3.4 g) caraway seeds, toasted and lightly crushed

2 whole cloves

1 cardamom pod, lightly crushed

½ cinnamon stick

2 thin slices fresh ginger

½ cup (100 g) sugar

In a medium saucepan, combine the apple cider with the spices and ginger. Heat gently over moderate-low heat for 15–20 minutes, making sure not to boil. Add the sugar and stir until dissolved. Remove from the heat and let the flavors infuse for up to 20 minutes. Strain the liquid and discard the spices and ginger. Serve in a warm mug.

The Larder

The heart and soul of the Mediterranean kitchen is inherent in this chapter. There are frequently used spice blends and pastes, pickled and preserved vegetables and basic sauces and stocks. Many of these elements are embedded in other recipes in this book. These are the building blocks that are essential to my style of cooking.

Ancient Arab Spice Blend

I wish I could tell you that this recipe dates back to the Ottoman Empire or a romantic story about how it came about. Truth is, I came up with the name for this spice blend on the spot after making it up for a chicken skewer recipe. It's very aromatic and pairs well with almost everything. I especially love it as a marinade for grilled meat and poultry.

ABOUT ½ CUP (45 G)

1 tbsp (4 g) coriander seeds

1 tbsp (6 g) fennel seeds

1 tbsp (6 g) cumin seeds

1 tbsp (7.7 g) black peppercorns

1 tbsp (7.5 g) caraway seeds

1 tbsp (8 g) Spanish sweet smoked paprika

½ tbsp (0.9 g) dried marjoram

½ tsp ground turmeric

In a small frying pan, combine the coriander, fennel, cumin, black pepper and caraway. Toast over moderate heat, stirring the spices occasionally so they toast evenly, for 2-3 minutes, until they start to warm up and become fragrant. Remove from the pan and let cool. Pour the spices into a spice grinder and finely grind in small batches. Combine in a small mixing bowl with the paprika, marjoram and turmeric. Keep in an airtight container for up to 1 month.

Tahini Sauce

Tahini, which is a ground sesame seed paste, is a magical ingredient. It often plays the starring role in many Middle Eastern dishes, such as hummus and halva, and there are a dozen or so variations of the sauce. In this recipe, it's meant to play the supporting role for more assertive flavors, so we keep it simple. The yogurt can be omitted by doubling the amount of lemon juice. Try it drizzled on roasted vegetables, or with roasted meats, fish and poultry. You can also use this recipe as a base and add other flavorings, such as spices or herbs, to it. Adjust the amount of water and acid accordingly. I prefer hulled and lightly roasted tahini to any other type, as the flavor and appearance are cleaner.

ABOUT 2 CUPS (473 G)

1 cup (230 g) tahini

1 tbsp (13 g) Homemade Thick Yogurt (page 189), or Greek yogurt

1 tbsp (15 ml) fresh lemon juice

2 garlic cloves, finely grated

¾ cup (180 ml) water, plus more if needed

Sea salt

Combine all ingredients in a medium bowl, season with salt and whisk until incorporated. The mixture will seize up at first and separate. You may need to add 1–2 tablespoons (15–30 ml) of water to get it to the perfect consistency, which is the consistency of thick cream.

CHEF'S TIP: A common mistake that I see people make with tahini is not stirring it well before using it. Since sesame seeds are high in oil content, when ground, the oil and the solids tend to separate. The solids settle in the bottom of the container. Be sure to stir the tahini very well, scraping the bottom of the container prior to each use.

Caramelized Paprika Butter

The paprika gets caramelized along with the milk solids from the butter, which intensifies the flavor and makes for a very vibrant red butter. I like using it as an accent, but it also works well for finishing cooked proteins or sauces. Just swirl a small amount into some potato puree or a pan-roasted piece of fish. Be sure to use really high-quality Spanish smoked paprika, preferably Pimentón De La Vera.

1½ CUPS (354 G)

1 lb (454 g) unsalted butter, cubed

1 tbsp (8 g) Spanish sweet smoked paprika (pimentón dulce)

½ tbsp (4 g) Spanish hot smoked paprika (pimentón picante)

In a medium saucepan, melt the butter over moderate heat until the milk solids just begin to brown and release a nutty aroma, about 5 minutes. Stir in the paprikas and cook for 30 seconds. Strain the mixture into a heatproof container. The butter can be refrigerated for up to a month. When ready to use, heat slowly in a saucepan or in a microwave.

Charmoula

This multipurpose North African marinade/sauce/condiment/dressing has complex flavors that, to me, exemplify the flavors of the region. Its versatility still amazes me; I'm yet to find a food that wouldn't benefit from a little charmoula.

ABOUT 3 CUPS (709 G)

¼ cup (37 g) garlic cloves

¼ cup (60 ml) fresh lemon juice

Sea salt

3 tbsp (18 g) cumin seeds, toasted and ground

3 tbsp (24 g) Spanish sweet smoked paprika

1 tbsp (5.3 g) cayenne

1 cup (67 g) cilantro, finely chopped

1 cup (67 g) flat-leaf parsley, finely chopped

½ cup (120 ml) extra virgin olive oil

1½ cups (360 ml) canola oil

In a blender, combine the garlic and lemon juice and season with a pinch of salt. Blend to a fine paste, scraping the sides of the blender as needed. Pour the garlic mixture into a medium bowl and combine with the cumin, paprika, cayenne, cilantro, parsley and both oils. Season with salt to taste and reserve in an airtight container in the refrigerator for up to 1 month.

CHEF'S TIP: You can reduce the amount of oil for a thicker charmoula. You also can add some water and lemon juice to thin it out a little if you are using it as a dressing.

Corn Stock

I hate wasting food. This is a prefect way to utilize the corncobs and make a delicious stock that can be used instead of vegetable stock, as a base for Sweet Corn Soup (page 63), or to cook Sweet Corn Farina (page 141), polenta or rice.

3–4 CUPS (700–950 ML)

6 ears corn, shucked, kernels removed and reserved for other use

4 garlic cloves, lightly crushed with the back of a knife

1 small yellow onion, roughly chopped

1 fresh bay leaf

Sea salt

Cut the cobs into quarters. Combine all of the ingredients in a medium pot with 9 cups (2.1 L) water, season with salt and bring to a boil. Continue to cook until the liquid is reduced by over half and has a strong corn flavor, about 30–40 minutes. Strain the corn stock and discard the solids. Can be frozen for up to a month in an airtight container.

Smoky Corn Stock

This smoky variation of the basic corn stock, lends a charred flavor that comes from grilling the corncobs. Alternatively, you could smoke the cobs and make the smoky flavor more pronounced.

3–4 CUPS (700–900 ML)

6 ears corn, shucked, kernels removed and reserved for other use

4 garlic cloves, lightly crushed with the back of a knife

1 small yellow onion, roughly chopped

1 fresh bay leaf

Sea salt

Preheat the gas or charcoal grill to high heat. Grill the corncobs over high heat, until they start to char and turn black, about 5 minutes per side. Place the onions on the grill with the cut side down, for about 6–8 minutes, until they are well charred. Remove the corncobs and onions from the grill and place on a cutting board. Once cooled, cut the onion into slices and the corn into quarters. Combine the rest of the ingredients in a medium pot with the onions, corn and 9 cups (2.1 L) water, season with salt and bring to a boil. Continue to cook until the liquid is reduced by half, about 30 minutes. Strain the corn stock and discard the solids.

Crispy Pita Chips

This recipe started out as a way to use leftover pita bread. Now I use them to garnish salads and soups, and to serve alongside dips and spreads.

8 SERVINGS

Canola oil, for frying or drizzling

4 (8" [20 cm]) pita breads, roughly torn into 2" (5 cm) pieces, or cut into desired shape

Sea salt

Sumac, za'atar or any spice mixture, optional

METHOD 1 (FRIED)

In a large, heavy pot no more than half filled with oil, or a deep fryer, heat the oil to 350°F (177°C). Working in batches, add the pita to the oil and fry until brown, turning constantly, about 2-3 minutes. Remove from the oil, gently shake off the excess oil and drain briefly on absorbent towels. Season with a small amount of salt and desired spice mixture, if using. Cool down completely before placing in an airtight container. Store for up to 3 days.

METHOD 2 (BAKED)

Preheat the oven to 375°F (190°C). Arrange the pita pieces on a baking sheet and drizzle with oil, toss to combine and season with salt. Bake until crisp and browned, about 10-12 minutes. Remove from the oven and season with the desired spice mixture. Cool down completely before placing in an airtight container. Store for up to 3 days.

Fresh Cheese

This is as simple as it's going to get for cheesemaking. I know that making your own cheese sounds intimidating. Trust me, it's not. If you can boil milk, you can make this recipe. This cheese is really a blank canvas. It's fairly mild in flavor, which makes it perfect for absorbing other flavors. Most of the recipes in this book call for the cheese to be crumbled. Alternately, you can press it for an extended period, say overnight, and cut it into slices or wedges, marinate it in olive oil and spices, similar to the Yogurt Cheese (page 191), or just eat it with a crusty loaf of bread with some honey.

ABOUT 3 CUPS (ABOUT 1 LB [450 G])

8 cups (1.9 L) whole milk

2½ tbsp (37 ml) distilled white vinegar

2½ tbsp (37 ml) fresh lemon juice

½ tbsp (4.2 g) sea salt

Prepare a colander with double-lined cheesecloth and set it over a large bowl.

Pour the milk into a large saucepan and cook over moderate heat until the temperature reaches 195°F (90°C), or almost boiling, while stirring continuously to prevent scorching on the bottom of the pan. Gently stir in the vinegar and lemon juice until the milk starts to separate. Remove from the heat and let stand for 10 minutes. At this point the white solid parts should be completely separated from the whey. Using a ladle, gently spoon the solids into the prepared colander; season with salt and let drain until the cheese is thick and most of the whey is drained, about 1 hour. Reserve the whey for another use. Remove from the cheesecloth and wrap in plastic film and refrigerate for up to 1 week.

Garam Masala

This north Indian spice mixture has become one of my favorite spice blends. It's versatile and not too overpowering. I like using it as an accent rather than the main flavoring ingredient, giving a warm spice note to any dish.

ABOUT ½ CUP (120 G)

2 tbsp (15.2 g) black peppercorns

2 tbsp (12 g) cumin seeds

1½ tbsp (6 g) coriander seeds

1 tbsp (7.4 g) white peppercorns

2 tsp (9.2 g) fenugreek seeds

1 tsp (4 g) whole allspice

1 tsp (2.2 g) whole cloves

4 dried bay leaves, crumbled

8 cardamom pods

2½ tsp (6.5 g) ground mace

1 tsp (2.6 g) ground cinnamon

In a small frying pan, combine the first set of whole spices and toast over moderate heat, stirring the spices occasionally so they toast evenly, for 2–4 minutes, until they start to warm up and become fragrant. Be careful not to over toast and burn. Remove from the pan and let cool. Pour the spices into a spice grinder and finely grind in small batches. Place in a mixing bowl. Grind the second set of spices finely in small batches and combine with the last set of ground spices in the mixing bowl. The final product should be a fine powder. If you have lots of chunks, simply pass through a fine-mesh sifter and re-grind the chunks. Be sure to mix the blend well. Keep in an airtight container for up to 1 month.

Ras El Hanout

This is one of North Africa's most essential spice blends. The name is Arabic for "head of the shop" or "top of the shop" and as the name suggests every cook and spice merchant has his or her secret and special formula. The most common attribute is the aromatic and layered flavor profile. I've tasted some spice blends that have upward of 80 different spices and some as simple as eight or nine ingredients. Each has its place when cooking. I think that 80 ingredients is a little over the top; I believe that some of the spices cancel each other out at some point. At Saffron, we've been adjusting this recipe for the past eight years. I think this is one of the most complex and intriguing ratios that we've done. It hits the palate on all levels—a little spicy, sweet, floral, bitter and earthy.

ABOUT ½ CUP (120 G)

3 tbsp (12 g) coriander seeds

2 tbsp (12 g) cumin seeds

1 tsp (3.4 g) caraway seeds

1 tsp (2.5 g) white peppercorns

1 tsp (2 g) grains of paradise

1 tsp (2 g) peeled dry orris root

½ cinnamon stick, crumbled

10 allspice berries

2 long peppers

8 whole cloves

1 black cardamom pod

2 tsp (1.9 g) dried rose buds

½ tsp (0.5 g) dried lavender

½ tsp (0.8 g) dried orange peel

1 tsp (0.9 g) saffron threads

4 green cardamom pods

2 tsp (4 g) ground ginger

1 tsp (2.6 g) grated nutmeg

1 tsp (2.6 g) ground mace

1 tsp (2 g) cayenne

2 tsp (6.6 g) ground turmeric

In a medium frying pan, combine the first set of whole spices and toast over moderate heat, stirring the spices occasionally so they toast evenly, for 2-4 minutes, until they start to warm up and become fragrant. Be careful not to over toast and burn. Remove from the pan and let cool. Pour the spices into a spice grinder and finely grind in small batches. Place in a mixing bowl. Grind the second set of spices finely in small batches and combine with the last set of ground spices in the mixing bowl. The final product should be a fine powder. If you have lots of chunks, simply pass through a fine-mesh sifter and re-grind. Be sure to mix the blend well. Keep in an airtight container for up to 1 month. Alternatively, you could use a mortar and pestle to pulverize the spices by hand. I'm sure it will bring unparalleled satisfaction, and maybe some muscle pain.

Simple Ras El Hanout

This simpler version of Ras el Hanout will suffice in a pinch.

ABOUT ½ CUP (120 G)

3 tbsp (12 g) coriander seeds
2 tbsp (12 g) cumin seeds
1 tbsp (7.7 g) black peppercorns
4 whole cloves

2 tsp (1.9 g) dried rose buds
4 green cardamom pods

2 tsp (6.6 g) ground turmeric
2 tsp (4 g) ground ginger
1 tsp (2.6 g) ground cinnamon
1 tsp (2.6 g) grated nutmeg
½ tsp (1 g) cayenne

In a small frying pan, combine the first set of whole spices and toast over moderate heat, stirring the spices occasionally so they toast evenly, for 2–4 minutes, until they start to warm up and become fragrant. Be careful not to over toast and burn. Remove from the pan and let cool. Pour the spices into a spice grinder and finely grind in small batches. Place in a mixing bowl. Grind the second set of spices finely in small batches and combine with the last set of ground spices in the mixing bowl. The final product should be a fine powder. If you have lots of chunks, simply pass through a fine-mesh sifter and re-grind. Be sure to mix the blend well. Keep in an airtight container for up to 1 month. Alternatively, you could use a mortar and pestle to pulverize the spices by hand. I'm sure it will bring unparalleled satisfaction, and maybe some muscle pain.

Se7en Spice

As the name suggests, this recipe has seven spices. For a region that has an endless number of spice blends, it always seemed odd that people refer to it as *Baharat*, which literally translates to "spices." Every household in the Middle East has its favorite proportions of the spices and some even have a different blend of spices. Use this as a guideline to create a spice blend that you like.

ABOUT ½ CUP (120 G)

3 tbsp (23 g) black peppercorns

1½ tbsp (11 g) cardamom pods

3 tbsp (36 g) whole allspice

1 tsp (2.2 g) whole cloves

1½ tsp (2 g) coriander seeds

1 tbsp (7.8 g) ground nutmeg

2 tsp (5.2 g) ground cinnamon

In a small frying pan, combine the black peppercorns, cardamom, allspice, cloves and coriander seeds. Toast over moderate heat, stirring the spices occasionally so they toast evenly, for 2–3 minutes, until they start to warm up and become fragrant. Be careful not to over toast and burn. Remove from the pan and let cool. Pour the spices into a spice grinder and finely grind in small batches. Place in a mixing bowl and combine with the nutmeg and cinnamon. Keep in an airtight container for up to 1 month.

Spice Salt

If you take nothing away from this book but this recipe, I won't be mad at you. Sprinkle it on your eggs in the morning or whatever you're having for dinner. Seriously, anything from steamed vegetables to fish or a simple piece of chicken can be elevated.

ABOUT ½ CUP (120 G)

2–3 tbsp (8–12 g) whole spice seeds (Any single spice or any combination will work. I like to use cumin, coriander, caraway or fennel.)

¼ cup (35.8 g) kosher salt

Toast the spice(s) in a small frying pan over moderate heat, stirring the spices occasionally so they toast evenly, for 2–3 minutes, until they start to warm up and become fragrant. Remove from the heat and allow to cool. Grind to a fine powder in a spice grinder and combine with the salt in a small bowl. Store in an airtight jar for up to a month.

CHEF'S TIP: Don't use any preground, store-bought spices for this recipe—or any other recipe, for that matter. Buy whole spices from a good source and toast and grind them yourself for the full effect.

Green Charmoula

This less common version of a lighter charmoula gets its flavor from adding more herbs and reducing the amount of red spices.

ABOUT 1 QUART (450 ML)

1½ tbsp (6 g) coriander seeds

1 tbsp (6 g) cumin seeds

2¼ tbsp (17.3 g) black peppercorns

¼ tbsp (2 g) Spanish sweet smoked paprika

1 jalapeño, seeded and roughly chopped

1 large green pepper, seeded and roughly chopped (about 1½ cups [220 g])

1 cup (67 g) cilantro, roughly chopped

1 cup (67 g) flat-leaf parsley, roughly chopped

1 Preserved Lemon rind (page 196), roughly chopped

2 garlic cloves, roughly chopped

3 tbsp (45 ml) fresh lemon juice

1 cup (240 ml) extra virgin olive oil

Sea salt

Toast the coriander, cumin and black peppercorns in a small frying pan over moderate heat, stirring the spices occasionally so they toast evenly, for 2–3 minutes, until they start to warm up and become fragrant. Remove from the pan and let cool. Pour the spices into a spice grinder and finely grind. In a food processor, combine the spices with the rest of the ingredients, except the oil, season with salt and pulse to form a paste, scraping the sides of the bowl as needed, and slowly drizzle in the olive oil.

CHEF'S TIP: This sauce is very different from its red sibling. The main difference is that this doesn't get better with time. It has a shorter life, 2–3 days at most.

Harissa

This North African spicy condiment is one of my favorite ways to add heat and spice to any recipe. There are many variations of harissa; here are two completely different types. The first is more traditional, using spices and dried chiles. I like to use a variety of dried chiles for a more complex flavor. The second is more of a roasted vegetable and chile paste that tastes fantastic on just about anything. I suggest that you try both versions side by side, as they are completely different, yet so similar. I love making rose-flavored harissa as well by taking the Traditional Harissa and mixing in ground dried rose buds and a few drops of rose water. My favorite way to use this is with yogurt and cooked beets to make a beet/yogurt/rose harissa dip.

Traditional Harissa

1-1 ½ CUPS (240–360 G)

---

3 dried ancho chiles, stemmed and seeded

3 dried chipotle chiles, stemmed and seeded

3 dried guajillo chiles, stemmed and seeded

2 tbsp (12 g) cumin seeds

1 tbsp (7.5 g) caraway seeds

1 tbsp (4 g) coriander seeds

1 tsp (2.5 g) black peppercorns

½ tsp cayenne

2 garlic cloves, roughly chopped

Sea salt

3 tbsp (45 ml) fresh lemon juice

2 tbsp (30 ml) extra virgin olive oil

2 tbsp (30 ml) canola oil

Put the chiles into a medium bowl, cover with boiling water and place a small plate on top to keep the peppers submerged. Cover the bowl tightly with plastic film and let soak until the chiles are completely soft, about 1 hour. Cover with more boiling water if they are not soft.

Meanwhile, toast the cumin, caraway, coriander and black peppercorns in a small frying pan over medium heat, stirring the spices occasionally so they toast evenly, for 2 minutes, until they start to warm up and become fragrant. Remove from the pan and let cool. Pour the spices into a spice grinder and finely grind.

Drain the chiles, reserving the soaking liquid. In a food processor or blender, combine the chiles with a few tablespoons (45–60 ml) of the reserved liquid and pulse to form a paste. Add the rest of the ingredients, except the lemon juice and oils, scraping the sides of the bowl as needed, until the paste is very smooth, about 5 minutes. Slowly drizzle in the lemon juice and both oils. Strain the harissa through a fine-mesh strainer and store in an airtight glass jar with a film of olive oil for up to 3 months.

CHEF'S TIP: I must admit, at the restaurant we toast the chiles in a dry pan prior to soaking them. Toasting the chiles heightens the flavor.

Roasted Harissa

The technique for this less traditional version is adapted from the kitchen of the magnificent chef Tim McKee, a mentor to me in my early career as a cook. The vegetables and spices cook slowly until they are soft and browned, allowing the flavors to meld together.

ABOUT 2 CUPS (400 G)

½ lb (227 g) fresno chiles, stemmed and roughly chopped

8 garlic cloves, peeled

¼ cup (66 g) tomato paste

¼ cup (63 g) tomato puree, preferably San Marzano

½ celery stalk, roughly chopped

1 carrot, peeled and roughly chopped

3 flat-leaf parsley sprigs

2 cilantro sprigs

2 fresh thyme sprigs

1 tsp (2 g) cumin seeds

1 tsp (2.5 g) caraway seeds

¼ tsp black peppercorns

1½ tbsp (23 ml) canola oil

Sea salt

Preheat the oven to 300°F (150°C). Combine all the ingredients in a heavy roasting pan, season with salt and toss to combine. Roast until vegetables are soft and deeply browned, about 2 hours, stirring every 20–30 minutes. Remove from the heat and cool completely. In a food processor or blender, pulse the mixture to form a paste, adding water to thin out if necessary. Scrape the sides of the bowl as needed, until the paste is very smooth, about 5–8 minutes. Strain the harissa through a fine-mesh strainer and store in an airtight glass jar with a film of olive oil for up to 3 weeks.

Lamb & Fennel Sausage

Inspired by the flavors of the fennel-studded Italian American sausage, this sausage is also amazing with a small amount of ground dried orange peel added to the mix. The sausage is delicately spiced but not overly spicy, making it a versatile recipe.

5 POUNDS (2.3 KG)

4 lb (1.8 kg) lamb shoulder, fat removed and reserved

1 lb (454 g) lamb fat, reserved from trimming the meat, or lamb belly

3 tbsp (18 g) fennel seeds

1 tsp (2 g) anise seeds

½ tsp white peppercorns

1 tsp (1.3 g) coriander seeds

½ tsp dried oregano

½ tsp chile flakes

2 tbsp (16.8 g) sea salt

½ cup (120 ml) dry white wine

Cut the meat and fat into 1" (3 cm) cubes and spread in a single layer on two parchment-lined baking sheets. Freeze the meat and fat mixture until very firm, about 1–2 hours.

Meanwhile, combine the fennel, anise, peppercorns and coriander in a small skillet and toast on moderate heat, stirring the spices occasionally so they toast evenly, for 2 minutes, until they start to warm up and become fragrant. Remove from the pan and let cool. Pour the spices into a spice grinder and finely grind. Combine in a small bowl with the dried oregano, chile flakes and salt.

Place the bowl of a stand mixer and meat grinder's parts in the freezer for 15 minutes. Set up the meat grinder with a coarse grinding plate. Place the mixing bowl below and grind the meat and fat mixture. Replace the coarse grinding plate with a medium plate and re-grind the meat into the chilled stand mixer bowl.

Combine all of the ingredients and beat in the stand mixer with a paddle attachment until well combined and a sticky mass forms, about 1 minute; be careful not to let the meat get too warm or overmix. Refrigerate for a minimum of 4 hours. The sausages can be refrigerated for up to 3 days or frozen for up to 2 weeks. If you would like to stuff the sausage in casing, follow the steps in the Middle Eastern Sausage recipe (page 193).

CHEF'S TIP: You can get medium ground lamb meat from a quality butcher. Ask for 20 percent fat content.

Homemade Thick Yogurt

I have vivid childhood memories of my mother making yogurt. It was a big deal. A lot was on the line when she would make the yogurt. I thought about it as a ritual. The milk had to be heated in a certain pan, stirred with a certain spoon and wrapped in a blanket before being placed in a warm spot next to the oven. Dare she catch you walking by that yogurt. If a batch didn't turn out, it was because the yogurt got "spooked" out. After preparing this recipe, I guarantee that you will never look at yogurt the same. The results of this recipe are superior to any store-bought yogurt and it lasts for about a month under refrigeration. Sure, you can put some fruit on the bottom of the bowl when you serve it. Always be sure to save some of the yogurt to make the next batch.

3–4 QUARTS (2.8–3.7 L) DEPENDING ON HOW LONG YOU HANG IT

1 gallon (3.8 L) whole goat, sheep or cow's milk

½ cup (100 g) plain full-fat yogurt (with live active cultures) at room temperature

Sea salt

In a small stockpot, bring the milk to a boil, stirring often. Remove from the heat and let stand at room temperature until the milk's temperature is 100°F–110°F (38°C–43°C) on an instant-read thermometer, about 20 minutes, while gently stirring occasionally.

Whisk the yogurt with about ¼ cup (60 ml) of the warmed milk in a small bowl; carefully pour the yogurt mixture into the milk in the stockpot. Cover the stockpot with plastic film and foil, transfer to an oven. Turn the oven light on and close the oven door. Let stand for 12 hours and up to 24 hours. The longer that you let it sit, the more sour it will become.

Remove the stockpot from oven and whisk in a pinch of salt. Place the yogurt in the fridge until it's well chilled. Carefully ladle the yogurt into a sieve lined with a double layer of cheesecloth; set over a bowl to collect the whey and refrigerate until much of the whey is drained and the yogurt is thick, at least 4 hours. Reserve the whey for other uses; I like adding it to tahini sauces instead of water and sometimes instead of lemon juice.

Yogurt Cheese (Labneh)

Growing up, we always had yogurt cheese in our fridge. It's excellent as a part of a traditional Middle Eastern breakfast along with Za'atar (page 202), olive oil, cucumbers, tomatoes and olives, or as a part of a composed salad, such as the Beet Salad (page 65). There are two variations to making yogurt cheese, one using homemade yogurt and the other using store bought. The first is the simplest.

Quick Yogurt Cheese

Be sure to use the highest quality yogurt that you can find. Avoid yogurts made with gelatin, pectin, food starch or any other thickening agents.

1 PINT (473 ML)

1 quart (950 ml) goat, sheep or cow's full-fat yogurt

Sea salt

Whisk the salt into the yogurt in a bowl and pour the yogurt into a sieve lined with a double layer of cheesecloth and follow the directions from the yogurt cheese recipe below.

Homemade Yogurt Cheese

1½–2 QUARTS (675–900 ML) DEPENDING ON HOW LONG YOU HANG IT

Homemade Thick Yogurt (page 189)

Make the Homemade Thick Yogurt, then hold the cheesecloth around the yogurt and then place a weight, such as a plate with some canned goods, over it. The weight will help draw out most of the whey. This can take up to 3 days. Gently squeeze out any excess liquid; the yogurt will be very thick and resemble soft goat cheese. At this point you can jar the yogurt as is or you can make yogurt balls by rolling the yogurt cheese into small balls, about ½ inch–1 inch (13 mm–3 cm) in diameter and place in a glass jar. Top with olive oil and herbs, spices, citrus zest or a combination of all three. I suggest that you experiment with your favorite flavor profiles. Cover and place in the refrigerator for at least 8 hours and up to a month.

Lobster Stock

This is a perfect way to utilize all of the lobster shells. You can add shrimp and crab shells to the mix if you have them.

ABOUT 5 CUPS (1.2 L)

½ cup (120 ml) canola oil

2 lb (907 g) lobster shells, preferably heads and legs, rinsed, roughly chopped

1 large carrot, diced

1 celery stalk, diced

1 large onion, diced

6 garlic cloves, smashed with the back of a knife

1 tsp (2.7 g) paprika

1 tsp (2.6 g) black peppercorns

1 tsp (2 g) fennel seeds

½ cup (120 ml) oloroso sherry

1 cup (250 g) San Marzano tomatoes, crushed by hand

2 fresh bay leaves

2 sprigs fresh thyme

1 sprig fresh tarragon

Sea salt

Heat the canola oil in the large pot. Add the lobster pieces and cook over high heat, stirring often, until they start to become aromatic and brown, about 7-8 minutes. Add the carrot, celery, onion and garlic, and cook over high heat, stirring occasionally, until the onions are slightly blistered, about 8 minutes. Add the paprika, black peppercorns and fennel seeds, and cook for 2 minutes, stirring often, until the spices are fragrant. Add the sherry and cook until almost evaporated, about 3 minutes. Add the crushed tomatoes and cook until any liquid has evaporated, about 5 minutes.

Add 4 quarts (3.8 L) of water and simmer over moderately high heat for 10 minutes, then reduce the heat to moderate low and simmer for 1 hour. Add the herbs and continue to simmer until the stock is richly flavored, about 30 minutes, skimming occasionally.

Strain the stock through a fine sieve and refrigerate until well chilled. If the flavor is lacking, return the stock to the stove and cook until it's reduced slightly and has a deeper lobster flavor. Season with salt.

Middle Eastern Sausage (Na'anik)

Also referred to as *makanek,* these are little sausages that are popular in the Levant, particularly in Lebanon. Although I don't drink alcohol, I cook with it and this recipe is a prime example of how just a small amount of cognac will alter a recipe in a drastic way if omitted.

5 POUNDS (2.2 KG)

1¼ lb (567 g) lamb shoulder, fat removed and reserved

1¼ lb (567 g) beef brisket, fat removed and reserved

2½ lb (1134 g) fat, reserved from trimming the meat, or lamb belly

2 tbsp (12 g) cumin seeds

½ tsp white peppercorns

½ tsp black peppercorns

1 tsp (1.3 g) coriander seeds

1 ½ tsp (3.3 g) whole cloves

1½ tsp (4 g) ground nutmeg

1 tsp (2.6 g) ground mace

2 tbsp (16.8 g) sea salt

1 cup (135 g) pine nuts, toasted (page 205)

¼ cup (60 ml) cognac

1 ½ tsp (8 ml) champagne vinegar

20 feet (6 m) sheep casings, optional

Cut the meat and fat into 1" (3 cm) cubes and spread in a single layer on two parchment-lined baking sheets. Freeze the meat and fat mixture until very firm, about 1-2 hours.

Meanwhile, combine the cumin seeds, white peppercorns, black peppercorns, coriander and cloves in a small skillet and toast on moderate heat, stirring the spices occasionally so they toast evenly, for 2 minutes, until they start to warm up and become fragrant. Remove from the pan and let cool. Pour the spices into a spice grinder and finely grind. Combine in a small bowl with the nutmeg, mace and salt.

Place the bowl of a stand mixer, meat grinder's parts and sausage stuffer (but not the stuffer tube) in the freezer for 15 minutes. Set up the meat grinder with a coarse grinding plate; place the mixing bowl below and grind the meat and fat mixture. Replace the coarse grinding plate with a medium plate and re-grind the meat into the chilled stand mixer bowl.

Combine all of the ingredients, except the sheep casings, and beat in the stand mixer with a paddle attachment until well combined and a sticky mass forms, about 1 minute; be careful not to let the meat get too warm or overmix. Refrigerate for up to 1 hour. If using the sheep casings, soak in warm water for 30 minutes. Drain and rinse the casings.

Set up the sausage stuffer and lightly oil the stuffer tube and attach it to the stuffer. Slide the end of the casing onto the tube and push it back gently, adding more and more of the casing to cover the length of the tube, leaving 2 inches (5 cm) at the end. Tightly pack the sausage mixture into the stuffing canister. Crank the sausage stuffer very slowly until the meat emerges from the tube and tie a knot at the trailing end of the casing. Slowly crank the sausage into the casing, making sure not to overstuff the casing. You want thin, uniform sausages for even cooking. Once you have filled the casing, tie off the other end and twist the casing to create 24-inch (10 cm)-long links. Repeat with the remaining sausage and casing. Refrigerate, uncovered, overnight. The sausages can be refrigerated for up to 3 days or frozen for up to 2 weeks.

CHEF'S TIP: Be sure to keep all of your equipment and ingredients very cold when making sausage, as the fat will start to melt and make for a not so sexy sausage.

Rich Lamb Stock

Although it is unorthodox to season the bones with salt for stock, I like to do so because it gives the stock a more rounded flavor. Be careful of over salting. Remember that you are going to reduce the liquid down by half, which is going to concentrate the flavor. We both know that you don't want a salty stock. Neck bones and shanks have a high collagen content, making them perfect for a rich and viscous stock.

ABOUT 1½ QUARTS (1.4 L)

Canola oil

6 lb (2.7 kg) lamb neck bones

1 (1¼ lb [567 g]) lamb shank

Sea salt

2 large carrots, halved

1 large onion, peeled and halved

1 small garlic head, split in half

1 tsp (2.6 g) black peppercorns

1 tsp (1.4 g) coriander seeds

2 fresh bay leaves

3 sprigs fresh thyme

Place a large roasting pan in the oven and preheat the oven to 450°F (232°C). Remove the pan from the oven and add a thin film of canola oil. Season the neck bones and shank with salt and rub with oil, then add to the roasting pan and roast for 25-30 minutes, until deeply browned. Turn the bones over and roast for 25-30 minutes longer. Transfer the bones to a large stockpot.

Set the roasting pan over 2 burners and turn the heat to high. Add 2 cups (480 ml) of water to the pan and deglaze, scraping up the browned bits from the bottom of the pan. Pour the pan juices into the stockpot along with 4 quarts (3.8 L) of water and simmer over moderately high heat for 20 minutes, skimming occasionally. Reduce the heat to moderate low, and simmer for 2 hours; add the remaining ingredients and continue to simmer until the stock is richly flavored and reduced by half, about 2 hours longer, skimming occasionally.

Strain the stock through a fine sieve and refrigerate until well chilled. Scrape the fat from the top and discard. If the flavor is lacking, return the stock to the stove and cook until it's reduced slightly and has a deeper lamb flavor.

Orange and Spice Marinated Olives

I believe that every meal should be served with olives. Take this recipe as a guideline; change the spices, herbs and citrus to your liking.

1 QUART (1 L)

1 tsp (1.4 g) chile flakes

1 tsp (2 g) fennel seeds, toasted and lightly crushed

1 tsp (1.3 g) coriander seeds, toasted and lightly crushed

1 cinnamon stick

2 fresh bay leaves

2 fresh thyme sprigs

Zest and juice of 1 lemon

Zest of 2 oranges

4 cups (560 g) mixed olives, different sizes, shapes, textures and colors

2 tbsp (30 ml) extra virgin olive oil

In a medium bowl, toss all the ingredients until well combined, then cover and refrigerate overnight so the flavors meld; keep refrigerated for up to 30 days. Serve at room temperature.

CHEF'S TIP: I sometimes eat these olives slightly warmed. Either pop them in the oven for a few minutes, or warm them up in skillet. They are especially fantastic alongside Yogurt Cheese (page 191) and a crusty loaf of bread for breakfast.

Pickled Shallots

This quick pickle is a magnificent accompaniment to many mezze spreads and rich meat dishes.

ABOUT 1½ CUPS (362 G)

3 large shallots, peeled and sliced into ¼" (6 mm) rings

1 cup (240 ml) champagne vinegar

½ cup (120 ml) water

1 tbsp (8.4 g) sea salt

1 tbsp (12 g) sugar

Place the shallot rings in a bowl. Bring the vinegar, water, salt and sugar to a boil in a small saucepan; pour over the shallots, cover with plastic film and let sit for 1 hour at room temperature. Reserve in an airtight container in the refrigerator for up to 2 weeks.

Preserved Lemons

Sure, it takes time to cure and brine, but the process is really easy. Make a larger batch and hold on to it. I promise that it's well worth the effort as it's an essential ingredient in *my* cuisine. The flavor of a preserved lemon is very distinct, bridging the line between slightly perfumey citrus notes and briny, slightly spiced sourness; it's a perfect balance. Traditional preserved lemons have a much higher salt content and most recipes don't include sugar or spices. I believe that the addition of sugar and spices helps flavor the brine, which I like to use as much as the lemons themselves.

5–6 LEMONS

1½ tsp (3 g) cumin seeds

1½ tsp (3.4 g) caraway seeds

1½ tsp (2 g) coriander seeds

¼ cup (45 g) kosher salt

1 tsp (4 g) sugar

5-6 lemons, rinsed and dried

1 cinnamon stick

½ cup (120 ml) fresh lemon juice

Toast the cumin, caraway and coriander in a small frying pan over medium heat, stirring the spices occasionally so they toast evenly, for 2 minutes, until they start to warm up and become fragrant. Remove from the heat and combine in medium bowl with the salt and sugar. Quarter the lemons, leaving them attached at the stem end. While holding the lemons over the bowl, generously stuff the insides with the spice and salt mixture, about 1½ tablespoons (7 g) per lemon. Tightly pack the lemons, cut side up, in a canning jar. Sprinkle extra spice and salt mixture between the layers. Add the cinnamon stick and cover overnight at room temperature. Add the fresh lemon juice to cover, leaving some space at the top for the lemons to release their liquid, about ½ inch (13 mm). Seal the jar and let the lemons stand in a warm place for 30 days, turning the jar upside down from time to time. To use, scoop the pulp, reserve the pulp and brine and use the skin according to the recipe.

CHEF'S TIP: These will keep for up to a year in the refrigerator. Don't worry if you see a lacy white film, just rinse it off before using; it's a part of the fermentation. I like to use everything that this recipe produces. The pickling liquid is added into stews, the pulp is pureed with some fresh lemon juice to make Preserved Lemon "Plazma" (page 199) and of course the skin is used all over ... I mean, on everything! I don't typically rinse the preserved skin, but if you feel that the lemons are too salty, I won't judge you for rinsing them.

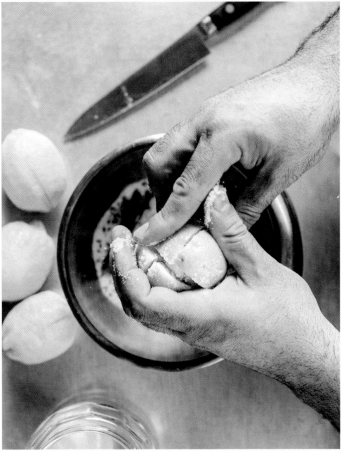

Rose Pickled Shallots or Pearl Onions

Serve these beauties with a selction of Orange and Spice Marinated Olives (page 195) and Pickled Turnips (recipe follows) alongside a spread of mezze.

ABOUT 1 ½ CUPS (362 G)

1 cup (240 ml) good-quality red wine vinegar

½ cup (120 ml) water

1 tbsp (8.4 g) sea salt

1 tbsp (12 g) sugar

1 tbsp (2.9 g) dried rose buds

3 large shallots, peeled and sliced into ¼" (6 mm) rings, or 10 oz (283 g) red pearl onions, peeled and halved

A splash of rose water

Bring the vinegar, water, salt, sugar and rose buds to a boil in a small saucepan, and add the shallots. Simmer for 1 minute, then cover with plastic film and let sit for 1 hour at room temperature. Finish with the rose water and store in an airtight container for up to 2 weeks.

Pickled Turnips

I know it's hard to think of a turnip as an exciting vegetable, but if this beet-spiked pickle doesn't change your mind, nothing will. An essential part of every mezze experience.

1 QUART (1 L)

1 cup (240 ml) water

2 tbsp (16.8 g) sea salt

1 tbsp (12 g) sugar

2 tsp (4.9 g) black peppercorns

1 fresh bay leaf

½ cup (120 ml) distilled white vinegar

6 small turnips, peeled and quartered (1 lb [454 g] total)

1 small red beet, peeled and sliced into ¼" (6 mm) rounds

In a small saucepan, heat about ½ cup (120 ml) of the water along with the salt, sugar, black peppercorns and bay leaf; stir until the salt is dissolved. Remove from the heat; add the vinegar and the remaining ½ cup (120 ml) water to cool down slightly.

Tightly pack the turnips and beets into a sterile glass jar. Pour the warm brine over to cover. Seal and let sit at room temperature in a cool place for 7–10 days. Refrigerate for 1 day before you use.

Saffron Water "Tea"

The most expensive spice in the world requires special treatment to fully extract its unique and almost-too-hard-to-pin-down flavor and deep orange color. When using high-quality saffron, a little bit goes a long way. In fact, too much saffron can ruin a dish with an overpowering, almost metallic, medicinal taste. When buying saffron, look for evenly colored, vivid deep red threads. Lighter colored threads or a lot of pale streaks indicate lesser quality. Avoid powdered saffron; you are paying for something that is probably adulterated or inferior in quality. Saffron needs moisture to release its flavor and color. The best way to extract flavor from saffron is to soak the threads in hot liquid. I prefer water, as it's neutral in flavor and can keep refrigerated for up to 2 weeks.

ABOUT 1 CUP (240 ML)

2 tsp (1.8 g) saffron threads

1 cup (240 ml) water or other liquid, warm but not boiling

In a small saucepan or skillet, while continually stirring, toast the saffron threads over moderately low heat for 20 seconds, until fragrant. Remove from the heat and crush the threads with the back of a spoon or using a mortar and pestle. Pour the warm water over the saffron and steep to release its flavor and color. Let the saffron steep for a minimum of 20 minutes.

Preserved Lemon "Plazma"

We came up with this anti-recipe at Saffron to use up all of the preserved lemon scraps. I felt terrible that we were wasting so many lemons just to get the peel, so this idea was born. Go ahead and experiment with it, but I must warn you: use it sparingly. A little goes a long way. Preserved lemon "plasma" adds a slightly bitter and very distinct briny-citrusy note to any dish. It's especially good as an addition to braising liquids or stews. It also makes a great base for a vinaigrette.

Pulp from Preserved Lemons (page 196)

Fresh lemon juice

Water

In a blender, puree the preserved lemon pulp with enough lemon juice and water to get a smooth puree. The puree should have the same consistency as applesauce. Strain through a fine-mesh strainer and reserve for up to a month.

Smoked Paprika & Toasted Garlic Vinaigrette

The aromas of the toasted garlic mixed with the paprika and sherry vinegar are a sure way to open up the appetite. I like to use this vinaigrette with everything from Marinated Peppers (page 47) to grilled seafood and meat. It's versatile, easy and delicious.

ABOUT 1½ CUPS (362 ML)

½ cup (120 ml) canola oil

½ cup (68 g) garlic cloves, thinly sliced

1 tbsp (8 g) Spanish sweet smoked paprika

⅓ cup (80 ml) sherry vinegar

½ cup (120 ml) extra virgin olive oil

Sea salt

In a small skillet or saucepan, combine the canola oil and garlic and cook over moderate heat, stirring continuously, for about 5 minutes, until the garlic is toasted and starts to brown lightly. Be sure to keep a close eye on it, as it can go from perfect to burnt in no time. If a few slices of garlic get too dark, remove and discard them. Anything more than that, throw it out and start over. Transfer the garlic and oil to a small bowl and let cool down slightly, about 1 minute. Add the paprika and stir in until fragrant. Whisk in the sherry vinegar and olive oil and season with salt.

Tahini Yogurt

This is going to be one of your favorite all-purpose sauces. It pairs great with vegetables, meat, fish and poultry.

2¼ CUPS (530 G)

2 cups (400 g) Homemade Thick Yogurt (page 189), or Greek yogurt

¼ cup (56 g) tahini

1 tbsp (6 g) black onion seeds (nigella seeds)

½ tbsp (8 ml) fresh lemon juice

1 garlic clove, finely grated

Sea salt

Combine all the ingredients in a medium bowl, season with salt and whisk until the mixture thickens. It should become a creamy paste similar to the consistency of thick cream. If necessary, add a few drops of water or yogurt whey to thin it out. Refrigerate for up to 3 days.

CHEF'S TIP: Tahini will thicken the yogurt. If you prefer the sauce to be looser, add a small amount of water.

Za'atar

When Arabs say za'atar, they could be referring to either this spice mixture or the fresh wild variety of hyssop or thyme. One thing that you won't hear anyone argue about is the health benefits of za'atar. Growing up, my father insisted that eating za'atar every morning would make me smarter. I'm not sure that it worked, but it sure was delicious! Za'atar is a versatile blend. It could be eaten on its own, with olive oil and fresh bread, sprinkled on salads or hard-boiled (my favorite breakfast) or fried eggs, served with Yogurt Cheese (page 191) or feta, used as a dressing or marinade, or made into a flatbread. You get the idea.

ABOUT ⅔ CUP (160 G)

3 tbsp (27.9 g) white sesame seeds

2 tbsp (4.4 g) dried oregano

1 tbsp (1.8 g) dried hyssop

1 tbsp (1.8 g) dried marjoram

3 tbsp (26.1 g) ground sumac

1 tsp (2.8 g) sea salt

Toast the sesame seeds in a small frying pan over moderate heat, stirring continually so they toast evenly, for 2–3 minutes, until they start to brown. Remove from the heat and allow to cool. Grind the oregano, hyssop and marjoram to a fine powder in a spice grinder and combine with the sesame seeds, sumac and salt in a small bowl. Store in an airtight jar for up to 1 month.

CHEF'S TIP: If you can't find hyssop, substitute it with dried wild thyme or oregano.

Brown Butter

This adds a nutty aroma and richness to any dish. I like to make darker brown, almost black, butter when it's being combined with other ingredients. If it's being paired with more delicate flavors, I like a lighter color.

1½ CUPS (344 G)

1 lb (450 g) unsalted butter, diced

In a medium saucepan, melt the butter over moderate heat, whisking occasionally, until the milk solids begin to brown and release a nutty aroma, about 8-12 minutes. Strain, discard the solids and reserve in an airtight container.

Clarified Butter/Samneh/Ghee

The process of removing milk solids from butter is very popular in Middle Eastern, North African and Indian cuisines. It can be made from cow or goat's milk butter, or a combination of the two.

1¾ CUPS (400 G)

1 lb (450 g) unsalted butter, diced

In a medium saucepan, melt the butter over moderate-low heat, undisturbed, until the milk solids begin to separate, about 10-15 minutes. Remove from the heat and let settle for 10 minutes. Skim the top and strain the golden liquid, making sure to leave the milky solids in the bottom of the pan. Discard the solids and reserve the liquid in an airtight container.

Cooked Chickpeas

I know how easy it is to open the cupboard and reach for a can of precooked chickpeas. This recipe will hopefully change your mind and give you a way to always have freshly boiled chickpeas at your fingertips. There is no need to soak the beans overnight.

ABOUT 6 CUPS (900 G)

2 cups (400 g) dried chickpeas, rinsed and picked over

Sea salt

Place the washed beans in a large saucepan and cover with cold water, about 2 inches (5 cm) over the chickpeas, and cook over moderate-high heat until they start to boil. Strain the liquid, and rinse the chickpeas under running water. Return the chickpeas to the pan and cover with cold water, about 2 inches (5 cm) over the chickpeas, and cook for 45–60 minutes, until the beans become soft. Season the chickpeas liberally with salt and cool them down in the cooking liquid. They can be refrigerated for up to 3 days. Alternatively, you can freeze them for 2 months in a freezer bag, making sure to keep them frozen in the cooking liquid. Thaw the bag under running water and use the chickpeas according to the recipe.

Roasted Tomatoes

2 lb (907 g) ripe tomatoes, cherry, plum or heirloom, halved or quartered

1 tsp (4 g) sugar

Extra virgin olive oil

Sea salt

Freshly ground black pepper

Preheat the oven to 275°F (135°C). In a large bowl, gently toss the tomatoes with the sugar, a drizzle of olive oil and season with salt and pepper. Arrange the tomatoes on a large baking sheet with the cut side facing up. Cook for 1–1½ hours, until the tomatoes are very tender and shriveled. Remove from the oven and let cool completely. Store in an airtight container for up to 1 week.

Fried Nuts

Growing up, this is the way that nuts were prepared at home: fried in a small amount of butter, ghee or canola oil. Pine nuts and almonds are amazing this way. As a matter of fact, this is the only way that I prepare almonds.

Heat ½ inch (13 mm) of neutral oil or clarified butter in a skillet over moderate heat. Add the nuts and cook, stirring continually, until golden, about 2-6 minutes. Use a slotted spoon to remove the nuts from the pan. Place on an absorbent towel and sprinkle with salt.

Toasted Nuts

This method is most commonly used in Western cuisine. It's not very popular in the Mediterranean because most home kitchens were not equipped with ovens. I believe that hazelnuts are best when roasted, but this technique works with all nuts.

Preheat the oven to 350°F (177°C). Spread the nuts in a single layer on a baking sheet. Cook until they are golden and have a strong, nutty aroma. Depending on the nut, it might take 10-20 minutes. Be sure to stir the nuts about halfway through for even cooking. Remove the nuts from the pan, season with a small amount of salt and let cool completely.

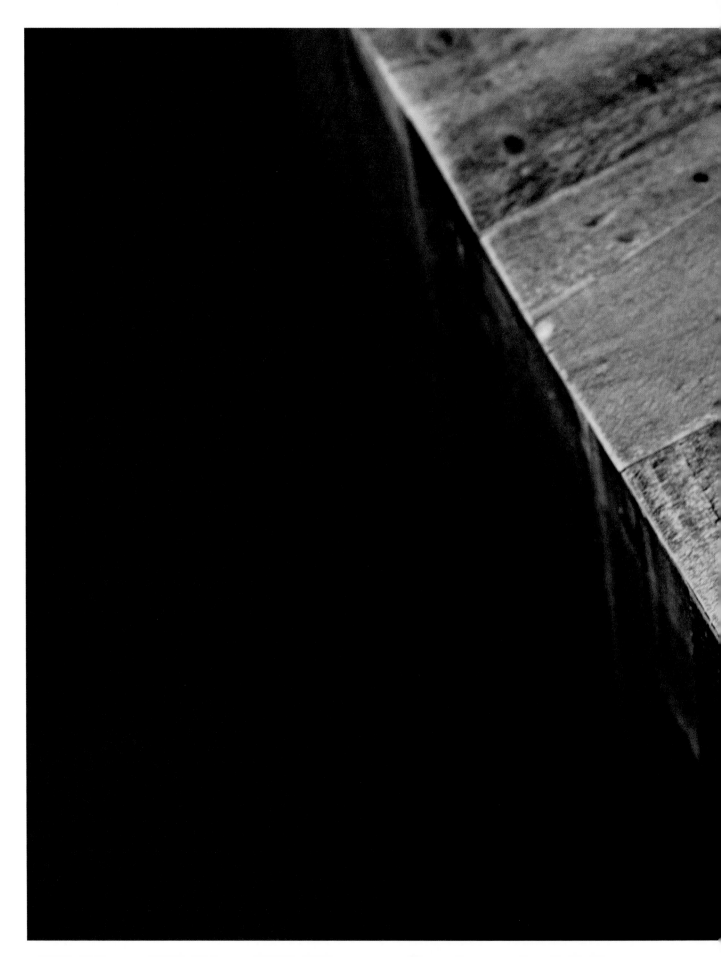

Acknowledgments

Thank you to the Saffron and World Street Kitchen family past and present for your devotion and for living my dream with me.

Saffron: Nick Altringer, thanks for helping test the recipes and cooking with passion. Amber "Grasshoppa" Wedell, I can't believe how much you've grown. Thank you for being such an amazing flour fairy. Jorge Garcia, you cook this food better than most, can you make more kubbeh, please? Also, thanks for cleaning up after me for years. John Williams, your passion for food amazes me every day, even when you played that *Star Wars* soundtrack for an entire dinner service. Cameron Borne, thank you for being a part of the family and for inspiring some of these recipes.

World Street Kitchen: Matt Eisele, your hard work and dedication are humbling. Thank you for running WSK the way I would. Swirl on, my friend. Jeremy "Fritzalicious" Fritz, your drive is astonishing. Thanks for being a master organizer in the chaos. Where is my prep list?? Ben Nieber, you make it happen on the truck—thank you for not crashing it. Also, keep stirring that chicken curry.

Maren Thorstenson, thank you for your love and constant support. I suppose I owe you an apology more so than thanks. I'm sorry my cookbook collection has taken over the whole house. UDABESSSS.

Geri Wolf, for your inspiration and fire. Thank you for all that you have done and continue to do. You amaze me.

Kathy Bakkenist, for your help getting the words out of my head and onto the paper. For your late nights of editing my poorly written intros. For being a champion eater. Your energy is motivating.

Matt Lien, for your soulful photography. It's hard to photograph a fish, when you can't ask it to smile. Your talent is humbling.

My publisher, Will Kiester, and the whole team at Page Street, for trusting me and giving me the freedom to do my thing. You rock!

My brother/business partner/motivator Saed Wadi, you believed in me before I believed in myself. I'm happy we took this journey together. I couldn't have done it without you. Also, thank you for not trying to edit this book.

Bill & Tony Nicklow, for taking a chance on a young cook. Bonnie & Tim Manley, for helping make my dream a reality. Kevin Manley, my first right hand man, it's so nice to see you grow. Jake Turner, for being you and for the goat poem. Chris Chang, for all the laughs and support, deeeis much! Andy Husbands, for passing on my information and the smock story. Mecca Bos, for being a true friend.

Finally, I would like to thank my mother and father, for encouraging me to pursue my dreams from a young age. Your support and love are the greatest gift.

About the Author

SAMEH WADI is the chef and owner of Saffron Restaurant and World Street Kitchen, both located in Minneapolis, Minnesota. He is nationally recognized as a multiple James Beard Award semifinalist for Rising Star and Best Chef Midwest (2008–2013) and by numerous magazines and publications, including *Bon Appétit* and *Food & Wine*. Wadi is an avid cookbook collector and reader and enjoys all things food-related. He lives in Minneapolis, Minnesota, with his cookbooks and spice collection.

Index

Asparagus with Duck, Gruyere Cheese and Saffron
    Vinaigrette, 71

Spring "Farrotto," 142